HOW LEADERS
LOSE THEIR WAY

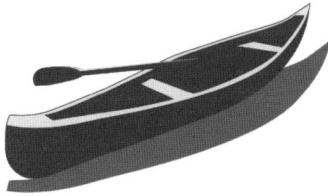

AND HOW TO MAKE SURE IT
DOESN'T HAPPEN TO YOU

PETER GREER AND JILL HEISEY
FOREWORD BY CHRIS HORST

ĩvp

An imprint of InterVarsity Press
Downers Grove, Illinois

InterVarsity Press
P.O. Box 1400 | Downers Grove, IL 60515-1426
ivpress.com | email@ivpress.com

Published in association with the literary agency of Wolgemuth & Wilson.

The publisher cannot verify the accuracy or functionality of website URLs used in this book beyond the date of publication.

Cover design: Faceout Studio, Addie Lutzo
Interior design: Daniel van Loon
Cover images: © vector_art via Shutterstock
Interior images: LeAnna Vine

ISBN 978-1-5140-1354-0 (print) | ISBN 978-1-5140-1355-7 (digital)

Printed in the United States of America ∞

Library of Congress Cataloging-in-Publication Data
A catalog record for this book is available from the Library of Congress.

31   30   29   28   27   26   25 | 12   11   10   9   8   7   6   5   4   3   2   1

FOR LARRY, JANICE, AND ALL THOSE WHO LIVE AND LEAD

WITH GREAT FAITHFULNESS

CONTENTS

FOREWORD

Chris Horst

A decade ago, when I collaborated with Peter Greer and Anna Haggard to write *Mission Drift*, we took a close look at what causes organizations to abandon their founding mission—describing just how common it is for institutions to lose their way. But what Jill and Peter have done in *How Leaders Lose Their Way* is the more uncomfortable work of replacing the microscope with a mirror. They've taken academic work and made it personal.

I've been on a similar journey in recent years as I've transitioned out of a long-held role at HOPE International. For most of my adult life, I had worked alongside Peter, Jill, and a team of colleagues who spurred me on as a mission-true leader. My academic understanding of these principles was solid at the time of my transition, but my internal response to leaving a workplace I loved revealed some gaps between what I knew to be true and how I actually lived and led.

I knew God was calling me to this transition, but after my departure from HOPE, when my emails slowed to a trickle and then to an almost imperceptible drip, I began to recognize that the overflowing inbox I'd long bemoaned had actually been a badge of honor. My insecurity over the lack of incoming messages revealed uncomfortable lies I had believed about my own identity and importance.

I now serve in a small, local manufacturing facility instead of a growing, global nonprofit. There are no built-in rhythms of prayer, worship, or devotions here. At HOPE, my coworkers were fellow believers. Now, by intention, I walk alongside many colleagues whose life experiences and beliefs scarcely resemble my own.

These dramatic shifts have forced me to examine how I experience and practice faith at work and in life. What should I hold on to and what should change in this new season as I live out my mission in a vastly different context? What was situational and what is foundational?

I've had to ask myself questions of purpose and personal mission. I've had to root out sources of false security. I've had to establish and practice the disciplines that ensure I stay mission true as a leader regardless of setting. Starting anew with this company, I've had to take an inventory not only of the organization but also of myself. Where are my loves disordered, my pursuits misguided, my defenses down?

We've all heard too many stories of leaders who've lost their way. We long for a different story; this book shows us how to live it. To ensure we finish well, we must face drift head-on, recognizing it and rowing against it. If you're in a season of transition, if your passion is growing stale, if you're pursuing purpose, if you want to finish well, then I'm glad this book is in your hands.

This book arrived at an important time for me, and I believe the same will be true for you. Jill and Peter offer us a mirror. What you see will cause discomfort and recalibrate you in all the right ways, and what you do when applying this book to your life will be among the most significant work you will ever do.

INTRODUCTION

WHEN MISSION DRIFT
BECOMES PERSONAL

Ten years ago, Chris Horst, Anna Haggard, and I (Peter) asserted in the book *Mission Drift*, "Without careful attention, faith-based organizations will inevitably drift from their founding mission. It's that simple. It will happen."[1] We detailed the surprising origin stories of organizations that lost their mission, including how modern-day pawnshops trace their history to a church outreach founded by the Franciscans, how the YMCA began as a Bible study and refuge for displaced young men, and how Harvard University was founded in 1636 with the mission, "To be plainly instructed and consider well that the main end of your life and studies is to know God and Jesus Christ." These institutions have endured, but they are not doing what they set out to do. They lost their way.

In the years since the publication, we've seen not only that drift has happened but also that it is happening with alarming speed and prevalence. Readers of *Mission Drift* have called or sent emails and letters to share additional case studies of drift. Without any effort on our part, we have a growing catalog of supplemental stories, each a disheartening example of a faith-based nonprofit, educational institution, or faith-driven company that moved away from its primary mission. We can affirm that organizational drift is pervasive—even more pervasive than we originally thought—with stories continuing to unfold in real time.

We've easily accumulated enough examples to populate a "revised and expanded" edition of *Mission Drift*. But as my colleague and friend Jill Heisey and I read and reflected on the stories that are and are not recounted within the pages of *Mission Drift*, we recognized that behind each account of organizational drift is a parallel story of leaders' personal drift, as they lost sight of their direction, purpose, or priorities.

Personal drift precedes organizational drift. Catalyzed by this discovery, Jill and I began to explore the question that's upstream from organizational drift: How do leaders lose their way? We shared this journey, though we've chosen to write in my (Peter's) singular voice for clarity and readability.

Too many well-known and admired leaders have lost their way. I've learned from their leadership best practices, and I wondered if I might not have just as much to learn from the challenges they've faced. How do leaders drift? And how could I avoid a similar outcome?

We wrote in *Mission Drift* about a pivotal moment when HOPE International, the nonprofit where I serve, recognized that we were in danger of drifting. We were, at the time, a small nonprofit focused on economic development in Ukraine. We used small-business loans and basic business training to help men and women break the cycle of poverty, enabling them to provide for their families and strengthen local churches. We had ambitious growth plans. Money was our primary constraint, but a prospective funding partner was offering to remove that constraint if only we would curtail our commitment to sharing the gospel. Saying no to this opportunity became a defining moment in my professional life as well as the impetus for *Mission Drift*.

That defining moment shaped HOPE as an organization by prompting a commitment to daily disciplines and decisions that help us stay mission true. Something similar will be required if we are to stay mission true as individuals.

Collectively, we have seen an alarming number of public leaders lose their way, fracturing families, causing organizations to drift, and harming the credibility of the global church. We've watched Netflix documentaries recounting egregious errors. We've listened to podcasts detailing the abuse of power and the harmful impact on churches and communities. We've read daily digests of the latest examples of fraud or mismanagement. We've grieved with those who have been hurt, and many of us have walked alongside friends who have personally experienced the fallout.

Yet are we paying attention? Are we taking the dangers of personal drift seriously? Drift happens subtly and slowly. Are we heeding the warning signs?

While high-profile stories of drift make headlines, a far more prevalent brand of drift is harder to spot: focus supplanted by distraction, faithfulness threatened by self-reliance, good things pursued as ultimate things. Our lives do not need to make headlines to tell a story of drift. Scripture reminds us, "Never be lacking in zeal" (Romans 12:11), but few passionately pursue their mission for a lifetime. Small compromises erode our faithfulness, and we realize—often too late—that what seemed like tiny shifts in direction significantly altered our course.

None of us are immune to drift. As Robert Robinson penned in the hymn "Come, Thou Fount of Every Blessing," "Prone to wander, Lord, I feel it, prone to leave the God I love."[2] When we acknowledge that we are prone to wander, we recognize that we would be foolish not to do everything possible to establish safeguards and commitments that help us stay mission true.

Ten years ago, we wrote from our conviction that organizational drift is real, seeking to equip the churches and charities we care about to stay on mission and be marked by long-term faithfulness. That remains true, but today Jill and I write out of our longing to see individuals, not just organizations, stay mission true. Our hearts and our prayers are for our families, friends, and colleagues—as well as ourselves—to be marked by long-term faithfulness.

While we've written to leaders, we define that term broadly as a function rather than a position. The principles in this book apply to readers in whatever sphere of influence they inhabit—home, community, church, or marketplace.

It takes focus, commitment, awareness, and an abundance of God's grace to stay on mission. We pray that this book will help leaders identify the beliefs, perspectives, and choices that lead to drift and encourage courageous course correction. Finishing well is no accident. If you desire to avoid losing your way in life and leadership, we are writing this book for you.

PART ONE

DRIFT IS
THE DEFAULT

1

THE DANGER OF DRIFT

*Let your eyes look straight ahead; fix your gaze directly
before you. Give careful thought to the paths for your
feet and be steadfast in all your ways. Do not turn to
the right or the left; keep your foot from evil.*

PROVERBS 4:25-27

It's been two decades since I heard my grandfather's wooden casket
clunk against earthen walls, but I vividly remember the details of
cemetery staff lowering his body into the ground. The graveside
service had ended, and our family overstayed, not yet ready to say
goodbye to this precious man whose prayers and life consistently
pointed us upward. My gaze lingered on a waiting backhoe that
hovered nearby.

The workers assigned the grim task of burying my grandfather
didn't know that he was the keeper of a thousand family memories.
They'd never witnessed his delight in tossing his grandchildren into

the air just to see them laugh, listened in on the ping-pong lessons he imparted, or glimpsed the sparkle in his eyes when he told a story. They couldn't have known the countless ways he had cared for his wife since the day they said "I do," or how this regal woman had collapsed in grief at the hospital saying "Don't you leave me, Jerold" as his soul left his body.

I knew all of that, and in the days following my grandfather's death, I learned still more. My grandfather spent his life shepherding a small Philadelphia congregation, impacting others' lives with little fanfare and great faithfulness. At his memorial service, those who came to remember him described how he prayed with conviction, played with joy, loved without judgment, and truly cared for people. In summary, his life was one marked by loving God and loving neighbor. He lived on mission and finished well. I have no doubt that he heard the words, "Well done, good and faithful servant" (Matthew 25:23).

Though I'd gained professional clarity on HOPE's mission some years earlier, my grandfather's funeral offered personal clarity. It forced me to follow the rather morbid recommendation of the sixth-century abbot Saint Benedict: "Day by day remind yourself that you are going to die."[1] My grandfather's life and death offered an invitation to pause and consider where my priorities and daily decisions might be leading.

While ministry was thriving, I was traveling too much and I was willing to do more. Growth and advancing HOPE's mission had become so important to me that I was regularly giving God and my family my leftovers. Time in prayer and study of Scripture was marginalized and—in practice, if not in lip service—less vital than all the "important work" I had to do. Evenings at home were sacrificed for nights on the road, sharing how parents in faraway places were able to invest in their children as they accessed financial services and experienced the hope of the gospel.

From the outside, perhaps I seemed to be thriving too. Nothing was obviously amiss or blatantly wrong, but in moments of honest reflection, I could recognize that small compromises had subtly recalibrated my course. My relatively minor scheduling decisions were, in the aggregate, taking a toll on my soul. I was working hard but losing my way, pursuing organizational growth strategies without similar intentionality around what mattered still more. Compounded by time, the gap between my current trajectory and a faithful finish was growing and would continue to grow. I was living the very definition of drift, and without conscious course correction, I was not going to finish well.

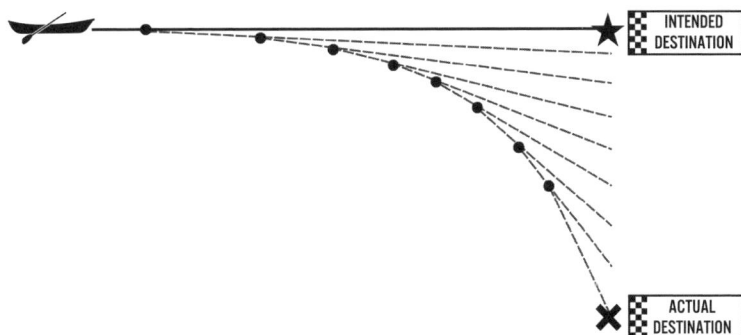

INTENDED DESTINATION

ACTUAL DESTINATION

ADRIFT

Leaders seem to routinely get caught in currents that pull them away from missional alignment. Whether it's happened to us, someone we know and love, or someone we've admired from a distance, we've all seen a leader *drastically, dramatically* lose their way as though caught in a rip tide.

We see Christian leaders with decades of service and thriving ministries lose their reputation and others' respect through a series of poor decisions. We read of business leaders who achieve the highest levels of prosperity but are caught in financial scandals and forced out in humiliation. We hear beautiful sermons about grace and love from the lips of those we later learn treated staff members abusively. We see pastors who dutifully shepherd their congregation while neglecting their own soul.

But we never think it will happen to us.

We don't stop to consider how we might be similarly at risk, as we play in currents without realizing their strength. Blissfully unaware, we wade into dangerous waters. Even when we spot drift in others, we still splash in the waves. Too seldom do we pay attention to the warning signs.

We live surrounded by currents that carry us to places we never intended to go, and currents have the same function as rip tides. They're less dramatic. They feel gentler and more innocuous, but they still carry us off course. Small acts of faithfulness or compromise determine our destination, and drift is all the more dangerous because it is subtle.

Although the twenty-four-hour news cycle may have heightened our awareness of prominent leaders' integrity failures and poor finishes, personal drift is neither new nor rare. People have sought to justify compromise since Adam and Eve found a way to rationalize that first bite (Genesis 3). A consistent theme of personal mission drift courses through Scripture, with faithful leadership as the exception rather than the norm. When leadership scholar J. Robert Clinton studied biblical leaders, he found that only 30 percent "finished well," which he defined as "walking with God in a vibrant personal relationship, developing the potential God has given to its appropriate capacity, and leaving behind an ultimate contribution that is both pleasing to God and established by Him."[2]

When Clinton applied the same criteria to more than twelve hundred historical and contemporary leaders, he reached the disturbing conclusion that "evidence from today indicates that this ratio is probably generous. Probably less than one in three are finishing well today."[3] Through conversations with friends who have vulnerably recounted their own stories of drift, I've come to believe that Clinton's assessment remains shockingly accurate. Drift is the default.

Feeling the pull in my own life, I wanted to understand what causes leaders to drift. Why those who start well don't always finish well. How rational people make irrational choices and even seemingly noble pursuits can lead us off course. Perhaps still more important, I wanted to understand what might keep us from drifting. Is there something fundamentally different about the one in three who finishes well?

When Jill and I thought of avoiding drift, we first thought of a boat dropping anchor. But the more we learned, the more we recognized the inadequacy of that illustration. At best, anchors keep us where we are. Anchors are not dynamic. To finish well, we'll need oars, not anchors.

ROWING ON MISSION

For a few years I lived near the Charles River in Cambridge, Massachusetts. As often as time allowed, I'd bike along the river so I could catch a glimpse of crew teams practicing. I've always been awed by the illusion of boats gliding atop the water as rowers plunge their oars beneath the surface in perfect synchronicity.

I've always wanted to try the sport, and on a recent summer day, Jill and I had the opportunity. Along with some HOPE colleagues, we donned matching crew T-shirts and looked the part when we arrived in Princeton, New Jersey, to spend a day on the water. First, we learned the basic mechanics on indoor rowing machines. It seemed easy enough. Yet within an instant of getting on the water, our unfounded confidence collided with our very unstable reality. It seemed any shift in body weight threatened to capsize the boat. The shell swayed precariously. Despite our instructors' uncommon patience and thorough explanations, our oars splashed and occasionally collided as we aimlessly meandered around the lake. Several hours into our lesson, at our peak performance, our boat lurched back and forth like a one-year-old learning to walk. We laughed a lot, overstretched our muscles, and developed a new appreciation for the skill rowing requires. Never again will we associate the word *effortless* with rowing!

Observing experienced rowers from a distance is deceptive. There is nothing easy about keeping the boat headed toward the finish line. Most of the time our little crew team was so consumed with the mechanics of rowing that we forgot to even consider where we were headed!

This experience became an object lesson in how complex and challenging an endeavor it is to stay on mission with far more at stake than a trophy or ribbon. Fixated on the mechanics of daily life and leadership, we can lose sight of where we're headed. From a distance, we might see people we respect living and leading faithfully. Perhaps it seems easy and natural, but it takes far more work than we might imagine to train our souls for a life on mission.

Living on mission requires clarity, dedication, and real effort. We can expect some awkward lurches, but knowing our destination and wholeheartedly rowing is the only way forward. Acquiescing to drift never leads to missional faithfulness in our organizations or our lives. If we desire to stay on mission, we must be prepared for courageous commitments and bold actions.

START WITH THE END IN MIND

My grandfather's funeral prompted me to ask, "Where is my path leading? And is that where I want to end up?" As one author wrote thousands of years ago, it is better to go to a house in mourning than to a house party because we live differently today when we keep the end in view (see Ecclesiastes 7:2).

A few months after the service, I sat down at my kitchen table one Saturday morning and penned my own eulogy. As I pondered what I hoped would be true of me at the time of my death, the exercise clarified what mattered most. What I wrote had nothing to do with professional accomplishments. In my eulogy, there was no mention of titles, jobs, or degrees. Instead, I wrote of relationships and gratitude to God and others. I wrote about the life that I would live if I were focused on remembering my Creator and living on mission faithfully to the end. It was shorter and simpler than I would have imagined, because as I focused on what truly mattered, so much of what I've striven for didn't make the cut.

The exercise could have been no more than a depressing way to spend a Saturday morning, but it became a significant moment. Sitting at the kitchen table, I wept as I wrote. For the first time, I had clarity on paper about what truly mattered. Perhaps the exercise was a little macabre, but it brought life into sharper clarity.

Writing my eulogy clarified the destination and helped me identify course corrections that I needed to make. Documenting my desired end slowly began to change the way I live.

DEFINING OUR MISSION

Focused on the impact I wanted to have at work, I was losing sight of my broader mission, to the detriment of my faith and my family. As I contemplated what it meant to finish well, I realized there were higher allegiances than my organizational allegiance—and this is true of every follower of Jesus. Our mission comes from Christ himself in the Greatest Commandment: to love God and to love others (Matthew 22:37-40).

This mission is, of course, broad. It doesn't tell us where to work or how to invest our time. But it does give us the framework through which every other decision must be evaluated. It says that we must rightly order our priorities if we are to live rightly, so we don't pursue good things at the expense of better things.

I'm reminded of a hierarchy proposed by the fourth-century Northern African bishop Augustine, who defined virtue as "the order of love"—or desires put in their proper place. Augustine argues, "We do well to love that which, when we love it, makes us live well and virtuously."[4] Only God meets that criteria.

When I finished writing my eulogy, I knew where I wanted to go, but course correcting is not a one-time activity. It continues to be a work in progress, as I live every day with the end in mind. Each year on my birthday, a calendar reminder prompts me to review my eulogy, reflecting on the past year and recalibrating for the next. I remind myself that my earthly life has an expiration date and then ask what course corrections are needed to finish well.

If we want to live on mission, we need clarity about where we're heading. It's easy to lose our way if we haven't defined our destination. Mission-true leaders know their destination.

ALIGNED ACTIONS

Once we have clarity on our destination, we also need to understand what will be required to bridge the gap between knowing and doing, aligning our actions and decisions with our mission, connecting what we do today with our eventual destination. Goals without tenacious commitments are almost never achieved. Staying on mission requires intentionality and discipline. It is rarely a gentle row down the stream.

The Charles River is home not only to many crew team practices but also to one of the world's premier crew events. Hundreds of teams compete in the Head of the Charles Regatta each October, and I've had the privilege of watching several races. Once, positioned near the race's end, I saw these athletes straining for the finish line, slumping over their oars in exhaustion once they had crossed it. Finishing well demanded their all.

We know that's not just true in rowing; it's true of any athletic pursuit. We expect it to be difficult and our muscles to be tired. We expect bruises and strains, and we know it takes preparation and strenuous training to compete. A lifelong New England sports fan, I smiled as I listened to Tom Brady's Patriots Hall of Fame induction speech. "To be successful at anything," he counseled, "you just have to be what most people aren't: consistent, determined, and willing to work for it. No shortcuts."[5]

We understand the same principle applies to music, art, and professional achievement, but too often, with our life's direction, we think it should come easily, naturally, or automatically. The reality is that living faithfully takes effort. "Is life less than a boat race?" Oliver Wendell Holmes Jr. asked. "If a man will give all the blood in his body to win the one, will he not spend all the might of his soul to prevail in the other?"[6] Staying mission true requires both clear direction and discipline. We must know where we're going and maintain the diligence to get there.

It also requires balance. When our motley crew team first climbed into our shell that August morning, we had not trained for rowing and were clearly not in peak physical condition. We had no clear direction and made no real progress toward any particular destination. But more than that, we barely stayed in the boat as we fought for balance. Several times, Jill and I felt sure we'd end up in the lake. Our instructor would comment that we were listing toward port, and we'd immediately overcompensate, pitching starboard.

Leaders face the same impulse. When we become aware of our tendencies and temptations, our natural impulse may be to lean so hard in the other direction that we still haven't achieved the balance that will allow us to live and lead on mission. We can go from treating a good thing as an ultimate thing (idolatry) to treating a good thing as a bad thing (disdain). Staying on mission requires balance, as we'll continue to explore in the chapters to come.

It's worth repeating: living on mission will not be easy, but soberly considering the impact of personal drift provides clarity on just how much is at stake.

LEARNING FROM OTHERS

Not long after writing my aspirational eulogy, I found myself listening to a leader as he shared a sharply contrasting story about a series of humbling experiences that derailed his life, family, and reputation. I had the utmost respect for his willingness to share, and, with remorse and tremendous self-awareness, he acknowledged the many small compromises he'd made. It wasn't one major mistake, he explained, but rather a long series of small, unwise attitudes and actions that led to a disastrous destination. It was unopposed currents, not a rip tide. It was drift.

As I listened to his story, it wasn't difficult to vicariously experience his pain. My friend and mentor Terry Looper often says that it always takes pain to truly change. While that is undoubtedly true, I've often wondered if it's possible to learn from the pain of others to avoid repeating their mistakes. In the words of author and leadership expert Jim Collins, "Better to learn from how others fell than to repeat their mistakes out of ignorance."[7] Perhaps feeling some measure of this leader's pain could prompt a change in me as well.

I imagined being in exactly the same situation, where my personal drift had devastated those I love most. I imagined losing my wife's trust. I imagined looking into my children's eyes and describing a series of harmful decisions I had made. I imagined the impact on colleagues and the loss of reputation and credibility. In truth, it wasn't hard to imagine.

Others' unwise decisions are an invitation to examine where (not if) we are making unwise decisions. The proper response isn't schadenfreude (taking pleasure in others' failures) or detached sympathy but humble introspection.

Each leader who has experienced drift could likely recount stories of others who lost their way. Too often, the problem is not ignorance but arrogance—believing it could never happen to us. Avoiding personal mission drift begins with an acknowledgment that *we* are prone to wander, that these stories could be our stories, that there is no immunity. "There but for the grace of God go I."

There is too much at stake to avoid diving deeply into the realities of drift and how it derails leaders. Our prayer is that this book will equip you to assess where you might need recalibration, shift your perspectives and routines, and develop the disciplines that will help you stay on mission. The end of each chapter includes prayers from our friend Ryan Skoog, as well as specific ideas and exercises to help in this pursuit.

Living on mission begins with a clear destination and the conviction that our finish line is faithfulness. Are you ready to do the work that will be required to remain mission true? If so, I invite you to grab an oar. Let's get ready to row.

PRAYER

Good Father,
>teach me the rhythm of returning to you, Lord and friend,
>again and again.

In hurried moments and rushed seasons,
>my heart has slowly slipped,
>little by little, without my notice.

Holy Spirit, reveal to me,
>show me how I've strayed from your path:
>in my thoughts
>in my desires
>in my attitudes.

(*Pause and listen*)

Holy God, draw me home.

Show me how I've strayed from your presence:
>in my schedule
>in my focus
>in my daily disciplines.

(*Pause and listen*)

Draw me back in kindness, in grace, in clarity and love,
>as you always do, as you always promise.

How enduring and persevering are your forgiveness and grace.

How merciful, how patient, you are with us, perfect Jesus.

—*Ryan Skoog*

FINDING OUR WAY—WRITE YOUR EULOGY

Writing your own eulogy is a profound way to clarify what matters most. What do you hope to be true about your life?

Picture this: Imagine attending your own celebration of life. What qualities do you hope friends and family members would recognize in you? Create a list of the people you would want to be present and the virtues, attitudes, actions, and mission for which you want to be remembered.

YOUR CELEBRATION OF LIFE	
Friends and family present	Notable virtues, attitudes, and actions

Put it in writing: Take time to write your own eulogy by following the prompts:

1. *From others' perspectives*:
   - What significant memories, milestones, or characteristics would be shared by your parents, siblings, spouse, close friends, children, or colleagues?
   - What attributes do you hope will be recognized?

2. *Your life's work*:
   - How do these contributions reflect your love for God and neighbor?

3. *Consider your fears*:
   - List a few things you fear could be said of you if you strayed from your mission. What do these fears reveal about any recalibrations God may be inviting you to make?

Review: Consider sharing your draft with a trusted friend or family member. Set a calendar reminder to read and reflect on your written eulogy annually. Place an object in a visible area as a prayer prompt to, "Teach us to number our days, that we may gain a heart of wisdom" (Psalm 90:12).

2

MEETING OUR MENTOR

Don't be impressed with your own wisdom. Instead,
fear the LORD and turn away from evil.

PROVERBS 3:7 (NLT)

A twenty-year-old rises to uncommon authority. He humbly recognizes his inexperience and limitations—as well as his influence—and seeks wisdom and guidance. He becomes supremely successful in business and trade, authors books, and is celebrated for his wisdom. He's respected globally, and leaders travel great distances to listen and learn from him. It's the quintessential success story: the stuff of leaders' dreams.

But in time it all begins to crumble. His ego grows along with his empire. His competencies and success lead to hubris. He seems consumed with building, achieving, and accumulating, as though he's simply unable to stop. He is plagued by greed and abuses his employees. People become a means to an end. With many acquaintances and employees but no real friends, no one helps this leader see how his pursuits are leading him off mission. He seems unable to find his way back to the humble posture that led to his success. His family fractures, and he dies with remorse and regret. It's a true tragedy: a leader who started well yet lost sight of his roots, relationships, and mission.

This story could describe the life of plenty of contemporary leaders. In fact, it sounds like the inspiration behind the pattern Jim Collins identified in his esteemed "Stages of Decline" in *How the Mighty Fall* (though Collins wrote of organizations, not individuals). But this tale isn't modern at all; it's the CliffsNotes of King Solomon's story in the Bible. Solomon's saga of grandiose success to epic failure provides the ultimate case study in personal mission drift.

In many ways, Solomon's life was defined by his ambitious pursuits. In his forty-year reign as king of Israel, Solomon accomplished a lot. He rowed hard after success but realized in his final days that his pursuits had undermined his mission rather than accomplishing it. He also failed to establish safeguards that would have kept him rowing in the right direction.

Solomon is far from the only biblical leader beset by drift, but Scripture offers a uniquely well-developed view of Solomon, with multiple sources exploring his life and legacy. The book of 1 Kings recounts Solomon's story from a contemporary perspective, while 1 and 2 Chronicles offer a historical perspective. We can compare the wisdom of Proverbs—written and compiled in the middle of Solomon's life, at the height of his intellectual and political power—to Solomon's late-in-life memoir, Ecclesiastes, written when the only thing left to tally was the true bottom line.[1]

With first-person insights, third-person observations, and the clarifying effects of time, we get a clear picture of where, when, and how this celebrated king went off mission. Comparing multiple sources, we can see both what Solomon knew and how he lived—and the wide chasm between the two. Reflected in Solomon's life, we see how easy it is to lose our way. To accommodate a growing gap between knowing and being. To drift.

Solomon's ancient story echoes with enduring relevance. We, too, struggle to connect knowing and being. As Solomon would say, "There is nothing new under the sun" (Ecclesiastes 1:9). But as we journey through the missteps of this leader, we have the opportunity to learn from his mistakes and avert some of our own.

HOW SOLOMON LOST HIS WAY

Around 990 BC, Solomon was born not only into privilege but also into a cautionary tale. Solomon's mother, Bathsheba, was already married when she caught the eye of his father, King David. David conspired to have Bathsheba's first husband killed on the frontlines of battle so he could take Bathsheba as his own wife. Despite David's repentance, his drift had real consequences (2 Samuel 11–12).

Solomon's genealogy was a reminder that it's possible to lose your way.

In the final days of his life, David counseled his son, "Observe the requirements of the LORD your God, and follow all his ways. Keep the decrees, commands, regulations, and laws written in the Law of Moses so that you will be successful in all you do and wherever you go" (1 Kings 2:3 NLT). David defined success for his successor: follow God.

Solomon started that way. Inheriting the monarchy with the blessing of both his earthly father and his heavenly Father (2 Samuel 7:11-16 NLT), Solomon worshiped God and recognized his need for divine guidance. Early in the young king's reign, God appeared to Solomon in a dream, inviting, "Ask for whatever you want me to give you" (1 Kings 3:5). In humility, Solomon asked God for wisdom, acknowledging that he was "only a little child," who did "not know how to carry out [his] duties" in leading God's people (1 Kings 3:7). "Who by himself is able to govern this great people of yours?" (1 Kings 3:9 NLT).

God honored Solomon's request, giving him legendary wisdom, wealth, and acclaim. But these good gifts became disordered loves. As Solomon grew in influence and renown, he lost sight of his mission to serve God faithfully and bless the nations of the world. Solomon adopted his own definitions of success as strong currents tugged at his heart.

Arrogance. Solomon began to place his confidence in his own abilities rather than God. His ego expanded along with the expanse of the kingdom: with success, hubris replaced humility.

Solomon penned proverbs warning of the dangers of arrogance, but he failed to heed his own warning as he began to drift from his God-given mission.[2]

Exceptionalism. Solomon seemed to have created an exception clause for himself. Given his stature, position, privilege, and wisdom, he operated as though he were exempt from the guidelines and guardrails that governed others. He led as if he possessed a royal "hall pass" permitting him to live outside the rules and restraints God established. God instructed, "Trust in the LORD with all your heart and lean not on your own understanding" (Proverbs 3:5), but Solomon trusted in his wisdom, routinely choosing his way over God's clear guidance.

God's words of instruction were given to help Israel's kings avoid things that would cause them to drift from their dependence on and allegiance to him: power, empire, self-reliance, and alliances that would compromise their distinctiveness. God took these instructions so seriously that he commanded the king to copy them in his own hand from the Levitical scroll, carry his personal copy with him, and "read it all the days of his life so that he may learn to revere the LORD his God and follow carefully all the words of this law" (Deuteronomy 17:19).

But Solomon didn't seem to think these protective commands applied to him. Rather than choosing rightly or reflecting and course correcting, he pursued his own way, overlooking or denying the potential consequences of his departure from God's intent.

Accumulation. Solomon seemed to believe that if a little of something was good, more must be even better. As Ecclesiastes 1:8 says, "The eye never has enough of seeing, nor the ear its fill of hearing." Solomon never had enough. He built entire cities dedicated to storing his possessions (1 Kings 9:19; 2 Chronicles 8:4-6), yet still he pursued more.

God instructed, don't take many wives (Deuteronomy 17:17), but Solomon was not a man of moderation and had seven hundred—plus an additional three hundred concubines (1 Kings 11:3).

God instructed, don't amass gold and silver (Deuteronomy 17:17), but "the king made silver and gold as common in Jerusalem as stones" (2 Chronicles 1:15).

God instructed, don't acquire great numbers of horses or return to Egypt to get them (Deuteronomy 17:16), but Solomon was drawn to power and control, accumulating twelve thousand horses from Egypt and Kue (modern-day Turkey; 2 Chronicles 1:14, 16).

Solomon's appetites were insatiable.

Acceleration. Despite asking God for the wisdom to choose *rightly*, Solomon chose *wrongly* time and again over the course of his reign. As his kingdom grew grander, Solomon repeatedly ignored God's clear leadership directives.

Solomon racked up a litany of accomplishments, living a life that most would deem wildly successful. He excelled at his job, enriching the royal treasuries, forming strategic alliances with neighboring nations, and achieving architectural feats like the First Temple and his own grand palace (1 Kings 3:1; 5:12; 9:10; 2 Chronicles 2:15-16). He "surpassed all the kings of the earth in riches and wisdom" (1 Kings 10:23 NKJV).

Yet what could have been perceived as success coincided with an acceleration of moving off course, leading to blatant expressions of abuse and idolatry. Solomon seemed to be winning, but he was losing his way. He excelled at his job but failed in his mission.

Abuse. To maintain his reputation and his kingdom's grandeur, Solomon imposed heavy taxes and forced labor on his subjects, leading to widespread discontent and unrest. Solomon seems to have neglected repentance, the course correction that could have restored God's favor. Instead, he secured trade alliances with marriage vows, then built pagan shrines to appease his foreign wives.

He built high places for the gods Chemosh and Molech on a hill east of Jerusalem, incontrovertible public evidence of his private drift. This king who began his reign with a commitment to God ended up worshiping foreign gods (1 Kings 11). Idol worship was, of course, not a new temptation for God's people, but it flourished during Solomon's reign, setting a precedent that most of Israel's kings followed.

There were both personal and national consequences to Solomon's drift. Speaking through the prophet Ahijah, God asserted he would tear the kingdom away from Solomon's descendants for Solomon has abandoned me and worshiped Ashtoreth, the goddess of the Sidonians; Chemosh, the god of Moab; and Molech, the god of the Ammonites. He has not followed my ways and done what is pleasing in my sight. He has not obeyed my decrees and regulations as David his father did. (1 Kings 11:33 NLT)

Solomon did not stay mission true. He lost his way. By the end of his reign, the thriving kingdom Solomon inherited was weakened. His policies had sown the seeds of division among his people and his choices displeased and dishonored God. Upon Solomon's death, the united kingdom of Israel split in two, creating the northern kingdom, which retained the name Israel, and the southern kingdom, known as Judah.

THE CONCLUSION

As he approached the end of his life, Solomon penned Ecclesiastes. With unflinching honesty, the king scrutinized his experience living life on his own terms, radically pursuing his own agenda. Rather than expressing satisfaction in his notable achievements, Solomon admitted it was a waste. Reflecting on his experiences, he shared hard-won wisdom, generally pointing readers in the opposite direction from the one he'd traveled. Living off mission, Solomon concluded that his pursuits were "meaningless."

Millennia later, Solomon's words offer us a chance to see today what we might otherwise realize only at the end. "Everything is meaningless . . . completely meaningless!" he wrote (Ecclesiastes 1:2 NLT). The Hebrew word *hevel* (pronounced hev-el), which our English translations render "meaningless," shows up thirty-eight times throughout the book of Ecclesiastes. That's a lot of meaninglessness.

Solomon ticked off his list of primary pursuits:

Achievement. *Hevel* (1:3; 2:11).

Pleasure. *Hevel* (2:1).

Wealth. *Hevel* (2:4-8; 5:10).

Control. *Hevel* (8:7-10, 14).

Power. *Hevel* (3:19).

Prestige. *Hevel* (8:10, 14; 10:7).

Legacy. *Hevel* (2:16, 18-19; 9:5-6).

Even wisdom, Solomon's one request of God: *Hevel* (2:15).

And just in case he omitted anything, Solomon reiterated in the final chapter of Ecclesiastes that everything is meaningless (Ecclesiastes 12:8). All the effort, all the striving, all the exertion is described as a fleeting vapor, a chase after the wind.

Strong's Hebrew Lexicon defines *hevel* as "emptiness or vanity; figuratively, something transitory and unsatisfactory."[3] A more literal translation of the word would be smoke or breath. It's ephemeral and elusive. The more we try to grasp or hold it tightly, the more we find it slips through our fingers. There's no substance to bear the weight of our longing for purpose and significance. We cannot make a mission out of *hevel*, but that hasn't stopped us from trying. We pursue affluence, experiences, and accolades without realizing that we pay an unreasonably high price for our fleeting satisfaction.

Reading Solomon's reflections in Ecclesiastes, we may be tempted to give him the epithet, "Wisest king, worst motivational speaker." A more nuanced read reveals that Solomon wasn't out to depress or discourage us in Ecclesiastes but to direct us. He was pointing us to a different path. Twenty-nine times throughout the book, Solomon clued us in to the parameters of his perspective, repeating the phrase "under the sun." When he said it's all meaningless, he was referring to our lives and pursuits apart from an intimate relationship with God: life the way he lived it. Life the way most people live it.

In the final chapter of Ecclesiastes, written in the final chapter of Solomon's life, he urged those who are young to remember God today, before our strength fails and our health fades, before opportunities evaporate and the end draws near. This is the time to consider our trajectory while we can still course correct. This is the time to allow the reality of God's eternal existence to change the way we live today. This is the time to actively pursue the path of missional faithfulness.

THE HOPE OF IRRELEVANCE

After mapping the course of decline ending in "capitulation to irrelevance or death," leadership expert Jim Collins concludes his book *How the Mighty Fall* on an upbeat note, arguing there is reason to hope because our destiny remains *in our own hands*.[4] But Jill and I believe there is reason to hope because it's not about "our own hands." For Solomon and for us, a grander story begins when we let go of the illusion of our own importance and self-sufficiency. We break with Solomon's example of moving from humility to hubris to eventual humiliation when we shift our focus "above the sun," beyond our misguided, self-centered pursuits.

We take our place in a grander story when faithfulness becomes more important than any other definition of success. We can recognize our limits, scrutinize our pursuits, and acknowledge our need for safeguards. Only when we accept our own irrelevance can we lead, as Katelyn Beaty describes, without "adopt[ing] the mechanisms and metrics of the world to fulfill kingdom purposes."[5]

It took Solomon a long time to recognize the gift of irrelevance. To get clear about his mission. To awaken to the currents pulling at his heart. To realize that he had been pursuing the wrong things.

We don't celebrate Solomon. He's more antihero than hero because, despite his accomplishments, he lost sight of his mission. Solomon's story is a tragedy, following the classic literary rise and fall. Who had a better beginning yet more tragic ending in Scripture? Still more tragic is the number of leaders who are familiar with Solomon's life story yet remain unaware that they, too, are losing their way, missing the warning signs in his example.

In Solomon's story and perhaps in our own, there are two paths to drift. The first is active. It's to follow our hearts, chase our dreams, and satisfy our appetites—even when our pursuits or our methods are misaligned with the mission to which God has called us. It's to chart our own course, expecting it to satisfy, consciously or subconsciously believing that our designs and strategies might work better than God's.

The second is passive. It's to pretend that we've stopped moving because we've stopped rowing. It's to deny that currents are, at every moment, acting upon us. It's to sit in the boat without engaging the oars, leaving our destination to chance. It's to fail to establish safeguards and loving boundaries, despite our propensity to wander.

The rest of this book will examine where Solomon went off course and how the pursuits and currents that affected him affect us still. We'll learn to clarify our direction, strengthen our disciplines, find balance amid unsteady waters, and establish safeguards to bind our wandering hearts as we row toward our mission. Solomon will be our teacher, though we'll also draw from examples of contemporary leaders to help us see the enduring applicability of Solomon's ancient lessons.

Jill and I heartily debated whether to include contemporary examples in this book. We believe the stories are instructive but have no desire to shame leaders who have drifted or disparage their ministries. After deciding not to include any recent examples, we spoke with a friend who pointedly asked, "Have you read the Bible?"

Scripture is filled with the stories of imperfect people, pointing us to another way. As fellow imperfect followers, we have much to learn from examples, both positive and negative. We selected the stories featured in the book not because we found these leaders' drift unbelievably egregious but because we found at least some element of their struggle relatable. Just as Solomon's memoir of Ecclesiastes is preserved as Wisdom literature, we believe there is wisdom to be found in exploring where other leaders lost their way.

As we reflect on others' misguided pursuits and vulnerabilities, Jill and I pray we see in them our own. May God, who works redemptively through brokenness, grant us humility and courage as we examine our hearts and pick up our oars.

PRAYER

Father,

You are the ancient, all-knowing, awesome God.

I admit I need wisdom; I need your guidance.

I lack understanding and need direction from heaven.

Awaken the spirit of wisdom in my soul.

Forgive me for the times I have been wise in my own eyes,

> the times I chose my own way without asking for your guidance.

Help me to not be wise in my own eyes.

Instead, remind me to sit at your feet,

> learning from the pure wisdom of heaven.

Teach me the serenity of your ways.

Teach me to surrender to your path.

May the wisdom of your Holy Word fill my mind.

May the wisdom of your Spirit fill my heart.

And when the wise path becomes clear,

> I ask for the humility to see it,

for the courage to take it,
for the faithfulness to keep it.
For your name, for your glory, for your kingdom forever.

—Ryan Skoog

FINDING OUR WAY—TAKE AN HONEST LOOK

None of us are immune to drift, but identifying drift helps us recalibrate and row toward long-term faithfulness.

Assess: Take time to honestly assess your heart. If you conducted a life audit in the areas Solomon identified as *hevel*, would it reflect faithfulness or drift? Use the illustration as a guide.

Shade the chart to reflect your self-assessment, based on the following scale.

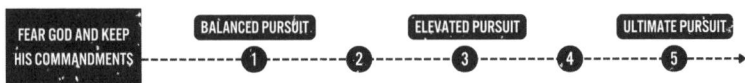

Respond: Based on your responses, where do you believe you are most vulnerable to losing your way?

Respond in prayer using these prompts:

- *Confess*: Which pursuits might you need to deprioritize so you can reprioritize fearing God and keeping his commands? Confess these before God.

- *Request*: Share your desires for redirection with God, asking for clarity where you may be off course and for courage to change direction. Pray through Psalm 139:23-24 (ESV):

  Search me, O God, and know my heart!
  Try me and know my thoughts!
  And see if there be any grievous way in me,
  and lead me in the way everlasting!

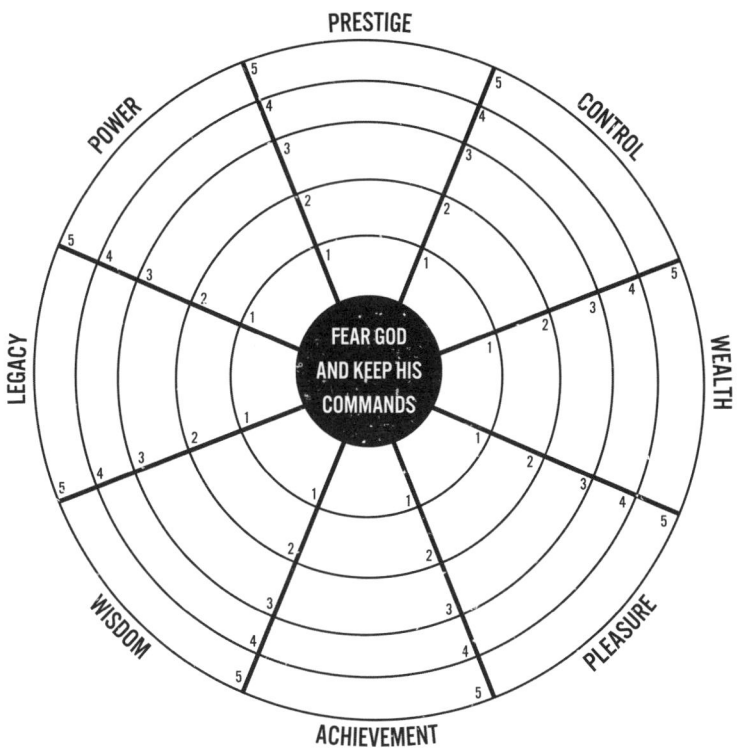

PART TWO

MISGUIDED PURSUITS

3

THE ALLURE OF ACHIEVEMENT

The greatest idol I find in leaders is ambition.

Brennan Manning

Waking at 2 a.m., I heard my wife, Laurel, rush to the restroom. Groggily, I entered the bathroom to rub her back while she bent over the toilet.

"Can I get you anything?" I offered. Hearing no response, I continued, "Cold towel? Pepto?"

"Please leave," she replied. No emotion in her voice. Just one very succinct request.

Back in bed, I thought about my upcoming trip. In a few hours, I was supposed to leave for California. But Laurel was sick and pregnant. Listening to the toilet flush repeatedly, I reached for my phone and started tapping out an email to cancel my trip.

But then, if I stayed home, what could I really do? I deliberated. Last evening, I'd already contacted someone to help with childcare.

Our friends would respond with chicken soup, and Laurel had a doctor's appointment the next day, where she'd be given antibiotics or whatever medicine she needed. Mentally running through my checklist of supportive actions, I concluded there was nothing else I could do. And clearly Laurel didn't want my help anyway. Besides, *I had to go* on this trip. It was a short, important meeting with individuals who could help us significantly expand HOPE's ministry.

Finishing my mental gymnastics and justifications, I nailed the dismount, arched my back, and extended my arms. Let's do this.

I deleted the email, rolled over, and fell back to sleep.

When the alarm went off a few hours later, I saw Laurel sleeping soundly. Confirmation. Getting up, I performed my well-rehearsed routine: silently showering, shaving, and making coffee in less than twenty minutes. I skipped the normal kiss goodbye—didn't want to wake her—and slipped out of the house.

In the car, I reassured myself. "I'll be back soon," I said out loud.

Opening the TED Talk app on my phone, I began listening to sociologist Dan Buettner's insights on how to live to be one hundred. Drawing from a study of regions where a high percentage of the population enjoys prolonged lifespans, Buettner shared how to live a long life. Oddly, none of the wisdom included prioritizing a business trip over caring for one's sick spouse. That's when it hit me. Live to be one hundred? I might not make it to next week.

Back home, Laurel felt abandoned after waking up to find me gone. "If you prioritized and cared for me, there is no way you would have left when I was sick, pregnant, and it was snowing," she later shared. Her message was sobering. There was simply no arguing who was right.

Choosing to go on the trip indicated a bigger problem: too much of my identity was bound up in my work. I was willing to pay a high price to "achieve." Leaving Laurel when she was sick sent a clear message: my most important mission is at work. I value my occupation more than our relationship.

EMPTY AMBITION

Sometimes the noble aims of our company or ministry exacerbate our pursuit of achievement, putting a sanctified sheen on our drift. What might be decried as workaholism is instead celebrated as "selfless service." We may be ambitious for good things, but does devotion to accomplishment honor God? What is it about our thirst for achievement that makes it so irresistible? It drives us, controls us, and, if we let it, transforms us into people we never thought we'd be. We focus on our goals but lose sight of our purpose. We work like our worth depends on it. Many leaders can relate, and no shortage have tried to warn us against following in their footsteps in pursuit of achievement.

At the end of his life, Thomas Aquinas, a great theologian of the Middle Ages, said, "I can no longer write, for God has given me such glorious knowledge that all contained in my works are straw—barely fit to absorb the holy wonders that fall in a stable."[1]

In the middle of his career, the great artist Pierre-Auguste Renoir said he had reached the end of Impressionism and realized that "I knew neither how to paint nor how to draw."[2]

Leonardo da Vinci summed up his brilliant career with the words, "I have offended God and mankind because my work did not reach the quality it should have."[3]

Influential British publisher and political theorist Leonard Woolf said this of his life and work:

> The world today . . . would be exactly the same as it is if I had played ping-pong instead of sitting on committees and

writing books and memoranda. I have therefore to make the rather ignominious confession . . . that I must have in a long life ground through between 150,000 and 200,000 hours of perfectly useless work.[4]

More recently, Robert Putnam, author of *Bowling Alone*, concluded that his prescient warnings hadn't prevented much strife. "I've been working for most of my adult life to try to build a better, more productive, more equal, more connected community in America, and now I'm 83 and looking back, and it's been a total failure."[5]

SUCCESS ON A DIFFERENT SCALE

Surely one of Solomon's StrengthsFinder attributes would be Achiever. In his early years, he seemed to possess boundless energy and ambition, and he knew unrivaled success in his work. At its apex, Solomon's strategically located empire reached all the way from the Mediterranean Sea to the Euphrates River in modern Iraq.

Solomon controlled the two primary trade routes, the Via Maris by the sea and the King's Highway farther inland. Anyone traveling those roads to do business had to pay tolls. The Phoenicians owned the seaports, but Solomon's status made him the majority partner in their trade alliances. He contracted the Phoenicians to build ships and send out multiyear expeditions to bring the world's treasures to Israel.

The king amassed flocks and herds and four thousand stalls for his horses (2 Chronicles 9:25). He built cities, erected military outposts, dug reservoirs, and planted groves of trees. "The scope of Solomon's grand achievement is indicated by the fact that everything occurs in the plural—houses and vineyards, gardens and parks, trees and pools," writes theologian and biblical commentator Philip Ryken.[6] His gardens, called *paradace*, inspired our English word "paradise." Ruins of Solomon's cisterns still exist millennia later, over a football field in area and thirty feet deep, capable of containing millions of gallons of water in that semiarid region. Solomon master-minded it all (or at least took credit for masterminding it).

He was also creatively prolific. Solomon penned more than a thousand songs himself (1 Kings 4:32), and as a patron of the arts, he hired musicians and singers to perform for him (Ecclesiastes 2:8). He was a combination of a legendary musician and producer all in one.

If anyone were to find satisfaction in achievement, it would be Solomon. But his work didn't satisfy him at all. "When I surveyed all that my hands had done and what I had toiled to achieve, everything was meaningless, a chasing after the wind; nothing was gained under the sun" he wrote (Ecclesiastes 2:11). He continued, "So I hated life, because the work that is done under the sun was grievous to me. All of it is meaningless, a chasing after the wind. I hated all the things I had toiled for under the sun" (Ecclesiastes 2:17-18). All that work and achievement wasn't enough.

He recognized at the end of his life that he had pursued the wrong destination, reaching what he thought was a successful life yet calling it all a waste. And it was, because Solomon didn't need to make a name for himself—he already had two names.

A KING WITH TWO NAMES

"Solomon" was only the first of two names given to Israel's future king. *Shlomo*, the Hebrew name David and Bathsheba conferred on their son, shared the same root consonants as the word *shalom*. Meaning "peace," the name communicated great hope for Solomon's future: that his reign would be marked by peace and prosperity, that he would be a successful king. But not long after Solomon's birth, God sent the prophet Nathan to give Solomon a new name: Jedediah, "beloved of the LORD" (2 Samuel 12:25 ESV).

In Scripture, names and identities were closely intertwined, and whenever God changed someone's name, it represented a significant calling. Abram became Abraham, the father of many nations. Sarai became Sarah, mother of nations. Jacob became Israel, no longer a deceiver but one who wrestled with God. But Solomon stayed Solomon.

It seems Solomon never embraced his God-given identity as Jedidiah. He went by the name his parents had chosen, and although his reign was marked by geopolitical peace, Solomon never found peace within himself. Instead, he vigorously pursued achievement: building the temple, expanding the kingdom, accumulating wealth and wisdom, and making alliances with foreign powers. None of these accomplishments brought peace to his heart or secured a strong finish. In the end Solomon realized he had chased the wind.

I wonder what kind of king Jedidiah might have been. How might Solomon's story have been different if he had embraced his other name—beloved? Perhaps recognizing his worth would have halted his endless pursuit of achievements and accolades. Perhaps believing he was fully loved would have allowed him to stop trying to earn God's favor or the acceptance of people. What if all Solomon's actions were rooted in his belovedness? That would have been a different king entirely.

BELOVED

Henri Nouwen was a brilliant scholar, prolific writer, popular speaker, and compassionate priest who wrestled with this same temptation to find his worth in his achievements. Despite acclaim, he constantly battled insecurity and doubt. He often felt restless, lonely, and unfulfilled. No amount of success brought satisfaction.

In his fifties, Nouwen left his teaching position at Harvard's Divinity School—a place where value was closely correlated with intellect and achievement—and traveled to Trosly, France, to serve as priest-in-residence among a community of intellectually disabled individuals. Nouwen was, as he put it just after his arrival, "looking for a community of people that could lead me closer to the heart of God."[7]

Over the course of that year and beyond, Nouwen uncovered the foundational truth of his identity. It wasn't what made him distinct or set apart from others but rather what is common to every human creation: he was the beloved of God. We are the beloved of God. He wrote, "Being the Beloved expresses the core truth of our existence."[8] For the rest of his life, this became the most enduring theme in Nouwen's writing and speaking. He discovered that his true identity was not based on his achievement but on God's extravagant grace.

The more Nouwen experienced this belovedness, the more he realized there was no going back to aligning his identity with his achievements. "As those who are chosen, blessed, broken, and given, we are called to live our lives with a deep inner joy and peace. It is the life of the Beloved, lived in a world constantly trying to convince us that the burden is on us to prove that we are worthy of being loved."[9] There was nothing to prove, no achievement to pursue, and no need to search for alternative identities. "Every time you listen with great attentiveness to the voice that calls you the Beloved, you will discover within yourself a desire to hear that voice longer and more deeply. It is like discovering a well in the desert. Once you have touched wet ground, you want to dig deeper."[10]

Nouwen recognized that ultimate meaning and satisfaction are found in belonging, not striving.

> Aren't you, like me, hoping that some person, thing, or event will come along to give you that final feeling of inner well-being you desire? Don't you often hope: "May this book, idea, course, trip, job, country, or relationship fulfill my deepest desire." But as long as you are waiting for that mysterious moment you will go on running helter-skelter, always anxious and restless, always lustful and angry, never fully satisfied. You know that this is the compulsiveness that keeps us going and busy, but at the same time makes us wonder whether we are getting any- where in the long run. This is the way to spiritual exhaustion and burn-out. This is the way to spiritual death.[11]

Over time, the pursuit of achievement will lead to one of two outcomes: constant striving or discouraged resignation, continuous climbing or aimless coasting. Those who think that the next ac- colade will be different from the last will continue their pursuit of achievement, often running roughshod over relationships and failing to love God and others well, in a quest to prove their worth. Others will succumb to the weariness of constant striving, feeling discouraged, deflated, inadequate, and decidedly off mission.

The only healthy way to break with our pursuit of achievement is to recognize that we are inherently beloved. While Abram, Sarai, and Jacob received their new, God-given names as adults, Solomon received the name "beloved" as a baby. Before he had achieved a single thing, God called him "beloved." The same is true of us.

For Solomon and for us, a message of "Keep trying harder!" will cause us to lose our way. Staying on mission requires effort, but our first effort must be to reframe our way of thinking, to recognize that entirely apart from our achievements, aspirations, and machinations, we are the beloved of God, who absolutely delights in his children: mess-ups, mistakes, and all. Listen for the still, small voice that says we are fully known and fully loved.

WALK AWAY

Earlier this year I heard an interview with basketball legend LeBron James. The interviewer asked James, "What are the qualities that make a great basketball player?"

"Discipline," James responded. Then he continued: "You have to sacrifice loved ones for a long period of time if you want to be great."[12]

James verbalized something many of us have experienced but few would put so bluntly. I cringe at the idea of sacrificing loved ones for the sake of achievement—yet I've done it too. In his statement, James set up a hierarchy: greatness above loved ones.

Our love for achievement fails Augustine's test of rightly ordered loves. Tim Keller expanded on Augustine's idea to show us how.

> If you love your work and career more than God, you will necessarily also love them more than your family, your community, and your own health, and so that will lead to physical and relational breakdown. . . . If you love anything more than God, you harm the object of your love, you harm yourself, you harm the world around you, and you end up deeply dissatisfied and discontent.[13]

But I still struggle to make courageous decisions that would rightly order my life and loves.

Recently, I met another Peter. He served the New Zealand Army for eight years. At graduation he was the youngest full lieutenant. He became the top student in his promotional courses for captain, and superiors described him as "an inspirational leader and role model." While we might expect courage from someone with his impressive credentials, to me, his greatest act of courage was in walking away to pursue his mission.

Newly married and expecting their first son, Peter and his wife, Jessica, saw the impact of deployments on marriages and families. Despite Peter's position, success, and potential, they decided he would step away from military service so that he could step toward family.

His next chapter was with a commercial diving school, where he quickly became manager and part-owner, training divers for the oil and gas industry. Peter excelled in the role, but once again his desire to achieve drove him toward work and away from his family. He shared, "After a few years in that role my oldest son said to me: 'Dad, when can we be a family again?'"

"I was heartbroken," he reflected. "The risk of being an absent father, which I had been attempting to avoid by leaving the army, had become a reality for my young son."[14]

Peter's wife, Jessica, could see that Peter loved his role and found respect and identity in it. But she felt the cost of his absence at mealtimes, when putting the kids to bed, and at family events. The job Peter loved was keeping him from being the father he wanted to be. Jessica knew what needed to happen but struggled to voice her conviction: "How many times can a man give up on his dreams for the family? How could I ask him to do that [again]?" she reflected. "Thankfully, children can be brutally honest!"[15]

Instead of justifying his decisions, Peter again summoned the courage to change course. "In very short order I left that role, sold my shares in the school, and became a student, looking at the impact of fatherlessness on the way that people relate to God as father."

Peter's clarity of mission empowered him to act decisively. "The foundational Christian mission, for every believer, is to love God, love others, and teach others to do the same," he says. As part of teaching others to do the same, Peter and Jessica have written their mission statement as parents of five sons: "To raise good men who love God, love their wives, are incredible husbands and fathers, and who look after the people around them." This conviction was "the filter" for the couple's decisions. It provided clarity and confidence that the financial costs and sacrifices associated with the decision to walk away from a lucrative business opportunity were worth it to live in alignment with their mission.[16]

Living as God's beloved, Peter and Jessica want to build their lives around sharing that same belovedness with others.

TOO HIGH A PRICE

Ambition frequently drives us toward empty accolades at the expense of people and purpose, and too often, it requires compromises. The pursuit of achievement remains as alluring today as it was for Solomon. Elevating the good of achievement, we are willing to make compromises to get there, justifying drift because of the nobility of our pursuits. But the ends never justify the means, and they often lead us into troubled waters.

Seeing our work in light of our ultimate mission to love God and love people means that we won't compromise people for profit. We won't sacrifice our closest relationships or integrity for achievement. We won't ask our families to pay the price of our ambition. We won't justify moral compromises for noble goals. We are invited to discover the antidote to our addiction to achievement: belovedness.

PRAYER

Holy Friend,

Help me run at the pace of your love,

    not at the pace of my ego and insecurity.

Let my joy be in serving you, not in accolades

    or accomplishments.

May your dreams become my dreams,

    your plans, my plans,

    your goals, my goals,

    your aim, my aim.

You see the two natures fighting within me:

    one wants you glorified at the expense of my personal gain,

    the other wants to personally gain at the expense of

        your glory.

Strengthen my resolve to live for your glory alone,

    your kingdom alone, your name alone.

I want to stay in step with your Holy Spirit, not ahead, not behind.

Too often I set out on your work, in my own way, in my own strength,

    and I forget you are with me.

May my work be worship unto you, may it bring me closer to you,

    depending on you, and lead me to knowing you more.

For you, the only righteous, holy perfect, true God.

—*Ryan Skoog*

FINDING OUR WAY—YOUR TRUER NAME

For most leaders, our identity is bound up in our achievements. Even our introductions generally center on our accomplishments and occupations. These are the names we embrace, as Solomon embraced *Shlomo*. But Solomon had a truer name, and so do we.

Reflect: What names have you embraced? List a few names, titles, or identities that come to mind in the word cloud.

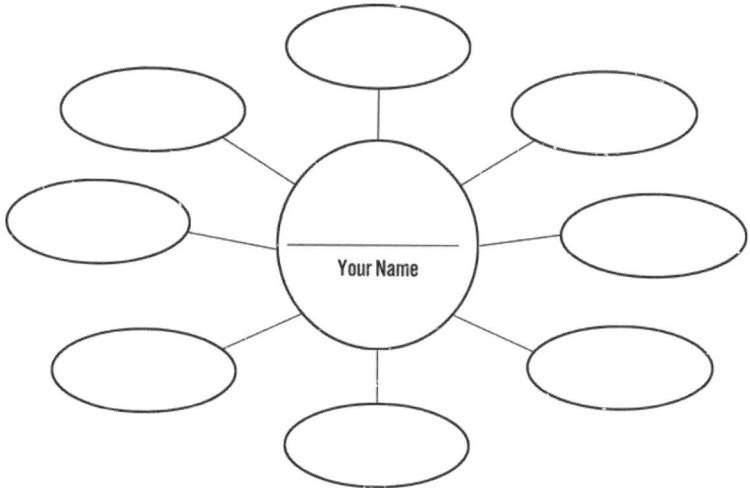

Your Name

Imagine: How would you feel if any of these titles no longer described you? If you no longer held the same role or title at work? If your role in your family or community shifted? If your capacity were reduced through age or illness? Which title or role would be the most difficult to lose? What fears arise in you when you think of losing that part of your identity?

Consider: Meditate on the truth of who you are in God's eyes in Zephaniah 3:17; 2 Corinthians 6:18; Ephesians 5:1; and 1 John 3:1. If your fears came true and you lost these parts of your identity, which identity would remain the same? What true name would you still bear?

Challenge: What would change if you rooted your identity in your belovedness? What would it take to make that change?

4

THE MASTERY OF MONEY

*If a person gets his attitude toward money straight, it will
help straighten out almost every other area in his life.*

BILLY GRAHAM

Jan and her husband, Paul, wanted to reach people around the
world with the love of Jesus. In 1973, they launched a small, part-
time TV station airing "a few hours of homemade Christian pro-
gramming each day" locally.[1] They invited partners to join them,
pleading not only for funds to keep the ministry afloat but for prayers
to empower it. From that humble beginning came the world's largest
Christian television network.

The couple became a fundraising powerhouse, bringing in
tens of millions in annual donations, most from contributions
of less than fifty dollars.[2] How they used the money was less
clear. MinistryWatch and Charity Navigator cautioned potential
donors that the ministry lacked transparency. Both Jan and Paul

netted disproportionately high salaries, but it wasn't just their salaries. It was spending sprees, private jets, and his-and-her mansions. It was ordaining staff members—including sound engineers and chauffeurs—to avoid Social Security contributions, branding homes "parsonages" to evade taxes, and financing a lavish lifestyle with tax-exempt money. Jan's excesses included a $100,000 motor home as an air-conditioned oasis for her pets,[3] renting a luxury hotel room for nearly two years for her beloved dogs, and remodeling the café inside one affiliated ministry three times in six weeks. When questioned, she allegedly replied, "No one has told me 'no' for 30 years, and you're not going to start now."[4]

In 2012, the couple's granddaughter and former finance manager blew the whistle on unlawful financial distributions. She said she had learned she was promoted to manage the ministry's finances because the family believed she would keep their financial misdeeds in the dark.[5] Instead, she let in the light.

The couple's lawyer justified the spending as "necessary to convey the ministry's position of accomplishment."[6] The ministry fired back with a lawsuit of its own against the granddaughter, alleging she, too, had misused funds. A second granddaughter brought a lawsuit against Jan, alleging that her concern for preserving the ministry's reputation led to her failure to report the granddaughter's rape at the age of thirteen by a ministry staff member. Both Paul, who died in 2013, and Jan, who died in 2016, were outlived by the lawsuits against them.

"Others may do things differently, and may criticize [the ministry]. . . . But what is absolutely clear is that [the ministry], with God's grace, has succeeded where most others have failed," the couple's lawyer asserted.[7] Is this really what success looks like?

TRAPPINGS OF SUCCESS

Brian, a pastor regularly featured on this Christian broadcast network, has also come under scrutiny for his relationship to money. Brian grew up as the son of a prominent Australian minister. For the first several years of his career, Brian worked in his father's church before planting his own in the suburbs of Sydney. When his father resigned from ministry, Brian merged their churches, creating a single megachurch known for its worship music, stage production, and charismatic theology.

The church blossomed, spawning locations in thirty countries and attracting over one hundred fifty thousand congregants. Brian rubbed shoulders with political royalty, signed book deals, commanded lucrative speaking honorariums, and lived an increasingly lavish lifestyle.

In 2023, the church captured the attention of one member of the Australian parliament, who alleged it broke financial laws in Australia and around the world, calling Brian out for his misuse of church funds. As evidence, he presented tens of thousands of documents compiled by an internal whistleblower.[8]

Brian denies legal wrongdoing, but is "legally permissible" the right standard for disciples of a humble, extravagance-eschewing King?

Even those who agree Brian crossed a line may dispute where exactly that line was crossed. Was it the Gucci sneakers?[9] The Cartier watch? The chartered private jets? The $150,000 tropical getaway?[10] How much luxury is too much for followers of Jesus? Does it make a difference whether our money is amassed through others' generous giving, our own ability to monetize ministry, or a for-profit company?

Whenever it happened, the conclusion is clear: the way Brian engaged with money pulled him off mission.

Jan, Paul, and Brian aren't alone in their pursuit of nice things. In 2019, Benjamin Kirby launched an Instagram account called PreachersNSneakers with its tongue-in-cheek tagline: "The Lord works in mysterious colorways." For five years, through nearly four hundred posts, Kirby called out luxury footwear, clothing, and other signs of opulence among pastors. Some see financial prosperity as proof of God's favor. Taking worldly riches as a sign of spiritual blessing, they openly flaunt their financial prosperity. Others have spoken up in their own defense: the items were gifts or purchased on sale. Does that make it better?

I can't answer that question, except to say that Jesus linked our heart and our treasure (Matthew 6:21).

MONEY AND MISSION

What is it about money that gets into our hearts and pulls us off mission?

Financial mismanagement is one of the easiest and most common ways to get derailed, personally and organizationally. The Trinity Foundation estimates that, globally, Christian religious leaders embezzled eighty-six billion dollars in 2024 and notes that "for over a decade the amount embezzled by Christian leaders has far exceeded the missions giving of churches."[11]

King Solomon again gives us a case study in the extreme. He knew the importance of a healthy relationship with finances. As Tim Maurer wrote in *Forbes*, "In only 31 chapters [of Proverbs], I found *more than 130 references* to things financial: money, riches, wealth, prosperity, poverty, and fulfillment beyond the material."[12]

Knowing and doing were disconnected when it came to Solomon's interactions with money, and his excessive wealth and possessions distracted him from God's commandments. He received tribute from other nations, controlled the dominant trade routes, and made silver and gold as common as stones in Jerusalem. He imported ivory, apes, and peacocks, creating a veritable zoo along with everything his heart desired. There had never been an accumulation of this much wealth in Israel's history. Solomon had gold reserves, twenty thousand horses, servants, a throne that was unparalleled, and so much more. He only drank from golden vessels and seemed to consider silver beneath him (1 Kings 10:21). He "excelled all the kings of the earth in riches" (2 Chronicles 9:22 ESV).

It came at a heavy cost. Years earlier God warned, "You may say to yourself, 'My power and the strength of my hands have produced this wealth for me.' But remember the LORD your God, for it is he who gives you the ability to produce wealth" (Deuteronomy 8:17-18). Solomon forgot that his ability to create wealth was a gift to be used in service to God and others. In hoarding and squandering wealth rather than stewarding it, Solomon did not follow God's design for money (1 Kings 10:14-29, Deuteronomy 17:16-17). In making treasure his heart's desire, he lost his way.

Solomon's yearly income was reported as 666 talents of gold (1 Kings 10:14, 2 Chronicles 9:13). At current gold prices, this would be over 1.5 billion dollars in annual income. Lest we lose the figurative significance of that number in the staggering literal value, 666 signified something deeper to the earliest intended audience of Jewish readers. Jews associate the number six with man and the completion of the physical world on the sixth day of creation. Repeating the number three times signified the ultimate, so the number 666 indicated ultimate physicality—akin to gaining the whole world but losing your soul.[13]

Andy Crouch speaks of money as "the most direct rival to God in human affairs."[14] He notes that many New Testament translations of Matthew 6:24—"You cannot serve both God and money"—leave Jesus' Aramaic word for *money* ("mammon") untranslated. He postulates that's because translators recognized mammon as no ordinary noun. It isn't just a principle or idea but a power, a nameable force with its own designs for humanity that are contrary to God's design. "When mammon really gets its grip into a human society . . . the result is treating persons like things," Crouch says.[15]

If we choose mammon as our master, we become its slaves.

Solomon built bigger barns, and when the barns were full, he built cities to store his stuff. He was a pioneer in the self-storage industry. Despite Solomon's massive wealth, he never made peace with his possessions. "Whoever loves money never has enough; whoever loves wealth is never satisfied with their income," he wrote in Ecclesiastes 5:10. "This too is meaningless."

It's easy to count what's in the bank but far more important to count the cost of what it took to get there. What price would you put on your mission? Your reputation and relationships? Your health? How much would you pay for the respect of your children and grandchildren? Despite Solomon's record-setting accumulations, his pursuit of wealth left him morally and spiritually bankrupt. It will do the same to us.

Near the end of his life, Solomon came to the same conclusion as so many others: wealth never provides meaning. It never satisfies. And it is never the ultimate destination of a life well lived.

It's amazing to read Solomon's words and recognize that nearly three thousand years later, we're feeling the exact same thing. We might not be drinking from golden goblets, but we have accumulated a shocking amount of stuff. Americans have doubled the size of our houses;[16] we have more cars than licensed drivers;[17] and to make ends meet we have full-time jobs, part-time jobs, and side hustles.[18]

We have so much stuff that the storage business is one of our fastest-growing industries.[19]

Our math works out to be something like this: Stuff + More Stuff + Even More Stuff = Extraordinary Happiness.

If that were true, Americans would be the happiest people on earth. But we're not. We're not even in the top twenty compared to other countries.[20]

Actor and producer Brad Pitt sounded more than a little like Solomon when he shared, "The emphasis now is on success and personal gain. I'm sitting in it, and I'm telling you, that's not it. . . . I'm the guy who's got everything. I know. But I'm telling you, once you get everything, then you're just left with yourself."[21]

The pursuit of wealth always comes up short, so how do we make peace with our possessions?

A GRACE-AND-GENEROSITY ECONOMY

Andy Crouch says there are two ways to wrest control back from mammon. The first is generosity, and the second is transparency.[22]

Brian got the attention of the Australian MP not only because of how money was spent in his church but also because of how it wasn't. While spending lavishly on its leaders, the church's expenditures for "people in need" reflected just "$2,900 for pastoral care direct costs, and $1,500 on pastoral care visitations."[23]

It's easy to throw stones at prominent leaders who have more to misuse, but the statistics show that selfishness and greed are trending. Often, the most generous among us seem to be those with the least to spare. Though higher percentages of higher-income individuals give, as a fraction of available funds, they give far less, averaging around 2 percent of income. Lower-income givers donate a far more generous 12 percent.[24]

Giving to charity is on the decline. In 2022, Americans spent 1.7 percent of their personal disposable income on charity, the lowest level since 1995.[25]

For all the money we invest in our own happiness, we're missing it. Long ago Solomon wrote, "A generous person will prosper; whoever refreshes others will be refreshed" (Proverbs 11:25). Studies confirm it: we become happier when we give. One study showed that people are happier when they are shopping for others than when they are shopping for themselves. Participants were given a small sum of money, from five to twenty dollars, along with simple instructions. Half the group was told to spend the money on others while the other half was instructed to spend only on themselves. Afterward, the people who spent money on others were significantly happier.[26]

It's the blessedness that God built into his grace-and-generosity economy.

Imagine the impact if Solomon had believed it was better to give than to receive and walked in that truth. Imagine what could have happened if he had invested his wealth in a mission aligned with God's heart to provide for the widow, foreigner, and needy. Imagine if he had used his wealth for the flourishing of all. Despite all that Solomon possessed, it doesn't appear that he ever experienced this type of generosity-induced refreshment.

MANGO GENEROSITY

Last year, I traveled to the Philippines. Before returning home, I loaded my suitcase with dried Filipino mangoes—my favorite food in the entire world. A few weeks after my return, I had the privilege of hiking a day on the Appalachian Trail with Alan Barnhart. Alan has long been a mentor to me, and he's among the most generous people I've ever met. Some years ago, he gave away his company to maximize generosity and he lives with an uncommon freedom, his family's lifestyle reflecting their belief that this life is not all there is.

As we finished a long day of hiking, we arrived at the shelter where he would be spending the night only to find every bunk occupied by other hikers. Alan was going to sleep under a picnic table that evening because all the beds were already taken. I wasn't envious of his accommodations. Before I said goodbye, I gave Alan one of the twenty packs of mangoes I had brought home with me. I thought this was generous, given how much I like mangoes. Alan seemed to understand the value of the dried delicacy in his possession. He thanked me warmly, "They're my favorite!"

What he did next astounded me. Alan had already hiked for many weeks with little access to food on the trail. It would have been prudent for Alan to stash the mangoes in his pack and enjoy a piece each day over the next week. In my mind, that would have been the rational choice and the path to maximum mango enjoyment. Yet that's not what he did.

In this shelter filled with hungry hikers, Alan tore open the bag of mangoes. Before taking a single piece for himself, he gave freely to each hiker in the shelter—those whose presence ensured he'd be spending the night on the floor. Watching Alan share his mangoes, it struck me that this was entirely consistent with how he lived. He didn't cling tightly to what was "his." He had a freedom to share generously with others. He had just received a gift, so how could he not share that gift with others?

Alan has broken the power of greed and discovered the joy of generosity. He stewards his possessions, right down to a bag of mangoes, in alignment with his mission to love God and love others.

A LITTLE ACCOUNTABILITY

Kevin Yan is the lead internal auditor at HOPE International, and he's passionate about his job protecting against fraud because he's deeply committed to HOPE's mission and knows that every misspent dollar is an "off mission" dollar. Kevin's intentionality around money has been shaped by the systems of accountability described in the Old Testament book of Ezra. Ezra's ancestor Seraiah had been the last high priest to serve in Solomon's Temple, which was destroyed 344 years after Solomon's death. In Ezra 8, the scribe and priest Ezra led a group of people tasked with transporting large amounts of gold and silver from Babylon to Jerusalem to rebuild the temple. They raised the treasures through voluntary offerings to the Lord and planned to use them to serve the Lord, not unlike a church or nonprofit today.

Kevin sees modern-day applicability in the internal controls Ezra established in Ezra 8 to mitigate the risk of mismanagement:

- The group fasted, humbled themselves before the Lord, and prayed for God's protection before they headed out (v. 21).

- Ezra appointed twenty-two people to be in charge of transporting the funds, creating shared responsibility and accountability (v. 24).

- Ezra weighed the treasure precisely and recorded the numbers predeparture (vv. 26-27).

- Ezra communicated that the treasure would be weighed again after arrival by a separate party (v. 29).

- The treasure was reweighed by others, ensuring it was accounted for and recorded (vv. 33-34).

Kevin shared, "I was touched by their clear sense of mission."[27] Because the mission mattered, transparency mattered.

How many of us live out a similar commitment to guarding the treasure entrusted to us—and guarding our hearts from the treasure entrusted to us? Systems of transparency and accountability are good for organizations and good for our hearts, but too often our money is shrouded in secrecy. We benefit tremendously from enlisting our friends to help us align our money with our mission to love God and others.

Transparency around finances is the second key Andy Crouch identifies to breaking the power of mammon in our lives. Crouch practices what he preaches—to the extreme. While he hasn't posted his personal financial statements online, he routinely opens his books to groups he interacts with in person. "Rather than just talking about our family's generosity in percentage terms I would put up graphs and tables . . . all with real numbers," he says. "When I do that consistently, people say 'I have never, ever heard a fellow Christian . . . tell me how much they have and how much they make.' . . . This should not be so. This secrecy that we have around these numbers . . . is a sign that mammon has its grip on us."[28] Recognizing that greed, hoarding, and mismanagement of resources flourish in the darkness, Crouch routinely shines a light on his finances.

Recently, a few friends of mine decided to try friendship-based accountability for their giving. They made a pact that begins, "We desire to follow God and invite each other to hold us accountable in the way we use our resources. . . . We will be open and honest with each other, seeking to provide counsel and encouragement to align our hearts and our wallets."

They open their "books" to each other, inviting questions and feedback. It's like getting a free recurring audit, minus the threat of penalties and prison. Sound scary? A little awkward? I agree, but I've witnessed how these friends are budgeting more wisely and giving more generously, simultaneously experiencing more joy and camaraderie in the process. They're aligning their money with their mission.

SEND YOUR HEART ABOVE THE SUN

Jesus said, "Where your treasure us, there your heart will be also" (Matthew 6:21). If that's true, I wonder where our hearts are. Perhaps they're in the garage, the house, the closet, or the investment portfolio. We place our money in the things we value, and our hearts follow.

Most of us have earthbound hearts, but we can send our hearts to a more secure location, above the sun, where moth and rust do not destroy and thieves do not break in and steal (Matthew 6:20). This runs counter to the classic temptations to grab the things we've not yet had the chance to enjoy. The luxury car, the second home, the boat, the season tickets. We become masters of rationalization, like my friend who said he felt a little check in his spirit before buying a luxury car. "But I got over it!" he chuckled.

Stewarding wealth calls for wisdom. Paul wrote to Timothy, God "richly provides us with everything for our enjoyment" (1 Timothy 6:17), but this is not a license to indulge but a challenge to give. The passage continues, "Command them to do good, to be rich in good deeds, and to be generous and willing to share" (1 Timothy 6:18). The whole world is yours to enjoy—so give as you've been given to.

Solomon and Paul invite us to consider that the joy of the new car will likely depreciate as fast as the vehicle itself. The boat might just be "a hole in the water," and the vacation home could take us away from church and community most weekends because now that we have it, we've got to get our money's worth. That's why Paul continues, saying that through generosity the rich "will lay up treasure for themselves as a firm foundation for the coming age, so that they may take hold of the life that is truly life" (1 Timothy 6:19).

Taking hold of the life that is truly life—isn't that what we all want? *Life that is truly life* is not something we can buy for ourselves, but it is something we can secure through generosity.

In light of eternity, what would it look like if we used our money on a grander mission than our own enjoyment? In service of our mission, money is no longer master or *hevel*. It becomes a good gift to be stewarded for God's glory. How many stories of financial mismanagement and personal mission drift might be avoided with a little more transparency, contentment, and generosity? How much joy might we discover from moments when we open our hands and enjoy mangoes together?

PRAYER

Father God,
You are infinite in power, and yet close as the breath in my lungs.
Remind me that you care about the cosmos,
    and at the same time my smallest needs.
Lift my heart above selfish gain.
Open my hands to freely receive, freely give.
May my eyes see with compassion
    and my focus be on others.
Help me give up earthly comforts
    for the infinite comfort of heaven.
Help me give up temporary wealth
    for the eternal wealth of heaven.
Mark my life with generosity:
    generous with my words,
    generous with my time,
    generous with my praise,
    generous with my resources,

generous with my gifts,

generous with my influence.

May you increase and I decrease.

Not my will but yours.

Not I but Christ.

May I always trust in you, Good Shepherd.

—*Ryan Skoog*

FINDING OUR WAY—
MONEY ON MISSION COVENANT

Use or adapt this covenant to help break the power of greed, unleash generosity, and serve God with your resources and finances.[29]

MONEY ON MISSION COVENANT

Lord, help me use the resources and finances you've given me for your purposes. Help me use my finances for a greater mission than the pursuit of my own plans, enjoyment, or comfort. Everything I have belongs to you.

Belief statements:

Everything I have belongs to God.

I am a steward, not an owner.

Generosity is God's antidote to greed.

Sin thrives in secret. I am committed to being transparent and open about my finances.

Spending, saving, giving strategy:

• I will allow myself $_____ in cash spending per year.

• I will allow myself no more than $_____ of accumulated wealth.

- My allocated giving targets this year will be:
    - ___% to my local church
    - ___% to _____ (other cause)
    - ___% to _____ (other cause)

I am committed to using money on mission for the purposes of God's kingdom and invite _____, _____, and _____ to walk with me in the way I use financial resources.

Signed: _____

Date: _____

5

THE PURSUIT OF PLEASURE

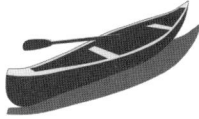

*There are two tragedies in life. One is not to get
your heart's desire. The other is to get it.*

George Bernard Shaw

Tony's mission in life was not just to create a great company; it
was to create happiness.[1] Over time, Tony's vision as CEO of
an online retailer morphed from customer happiness, to employee
happiness, to "delivering happiness to the world."[2]

Happiness mattered so much to Tony that he titled his 2010
memoir/business treatise *Delivering Happiness: A Path to Profits,
Passion, and Purpose.*

An entrepreneur at heart, Tony founded or grew multiple companies, including a first-of-its-kind online shoe retailer. Eager to
build the right team, he offered generous quitting bonuses to employees who determined early on that the company was not the
right fit for them. Later, to promote workplace happiness, Tony

experimented for a time with abolishing conventional reporting structures, hierarchies, and job titles. Although that experiment proved largely unsuccessful, Tony's company was routinely recognized as a great workplace.

Other leaders were eager to learn from Tony, so he established an online platform to host two-day seminars on value setting and culture building. Leaders around the world flocked to learn. Though Tony ran what began as an online shoe store, "He was never interested in shoes," says Fred Mossler, a former executive of the company. "Tony's journey was to improve the human condition."[3]

Tony's pursuit of happiness frequently blurred the lines of professionalism, beginning with a San Francisco penthouse that served as the company's party hub and rent-free employee housing complex.[4] Rather than work-life balance, Tony espoused work-life integration.[5] "The parties were nearly constant, and [Tony] even had his own signature drink—shots of a herbaceous Italian spirit, Fernet—that he would imbibe anytime, with visiting clients, journalists or seemingly anyone," reported journalists Angel Au-Yeung and David Jeans.[6]

Tony moved the retailer's headquarters to Las Vegas in 2004 and invested heavily to transform the local community, creating a city within a city where employees both worked and socialized. When Tony got stuck in Park City, Utah, early in the Covid pandemic, he stayed and attempted to create a similar enclave there. For any who were willing to relocate to join him in Park City, Tony offered to double their highest-ever salary. All they had to do was "be happy."[7] "His desire to achieve happiness, and especially to spread it to those around him, was so great that he staked his entire career, and his livelihood, on that goal," wrote journalists Kirsten Grind and Katherine Sayre. "It was his life's mission, and it was ultimately his downfall."[8]

Late in 2020, at just forty-six years old, Tony died of smoke inhalation from a suspicious house fire. In the aftermath, unsettling details of his final months began to come to light. The world learned how he abused drugs and cut off long-standing friends and family members who tried to intervene, all while trying to build a Disneyland 2.0, complete with the world's largest hot air balloon collection.[9] A letter Tony received from the singer Jewel, made public after his death, asserted, "The people you are surrounding yourself with are either ignorant or willing to be complicit in you killing yourself. . . . When you look around and realize that every single person around you is on your payroll, then you are in trouble."[10]

A 2010 interview might have foreshadowed problems, re-creating a scene that could have come straight from Solomon's life. "I have to ask," said interviewer Kai Ryssdal. "You're running a billion-dollar company, you've got a book on the *New York Times* best seller list, by all accounts incredibly successful. . . . Are you happy?"

In response, a decade before his tragic death, Tony seems to recognize that happiness is fleeting, ephemeral, or, in the words of Ecclesiastes, *hevel*. "Yeah, well it's one of those things where happiness is much more about progress than it is about achievement. . . . It's not something that once you achieve it, then you automatically have it forever. It's not a destination, it's ongoing."[11]

Like Solomon before him, Tony never found the happiness he desired, though he chased pleasure until his dying day. He never completed his vision for Disneyland 2.0, but even if he had, Tony would have confirmed what he already knew to be true: happiness isn't a destination.

SEEKING THE MAGICAL KINGDOM

Our shared longing for a magical kingdom has spurred many a pilgrimage to one coast or the other for a foretaste of happily ever after. Walt Disney himself proclaimed his theme park "the happiest place on earth."

I remember my first visit to the Magic Kingdom. I was accompanied by Lili, my then-eight-year-old daughter. We both were excited: Lili to meet the cast and characters and me to create a lifelong memory with my daughter.

During a tour of an on-grounds museum, we saw the original bench from Griffith Park in Los Angeles where the idea of Disneyland was born. As Disney watched his young daughters play on a merry-go-round, he envisioned a carefree haven where parents and children could have fun together, a place that would fulfill the universal longing for a kingdom of happiness. As author Al Hsu wrote, "The Magic Kingdom is humanity's best attempt at replicating a heavenly kingdom. And yet the tragedy of this fairy tale is that the Magic Kingdom falls far short of the kingdom of God."[12]

We quickly realize that the happiest place on earth isn't always happy.

I heard a child begging for cotton candy while licking an ice cream cone. I observed a mother chastising her overstimulated children on the verge of meltdown, "You're supposed to be happy!" I saw dads transfixed by the phones in their hands, oblivious to the children by their feet; families in tight spaces agitated by long lines; employees biting their tongues with cranky customers.

Just another day in paradise.

You don't need to be a theologian to realize that if Disneyland is the happiest place on earth, it's only an indictment of the planet. Lili and I walked away with some special memories, along with tired legs, expensive souvenirs, and no reason to believe that we'll find what we long for at Disney. What is it about our pursuit of pleasure that pulls us off course?

BUILDING UTOPIA

Long before Walt Disney dreamed of a Magic Kingdom, King Solomon set to work designing his own under-the-sun utopia.

> I undertook great projects: I built houses for myself and planted vineyards. I made gardens and parks and planted all kinds of fruit trees in them. I made reservoirs to water groves of flourishing trees. I bought male and female slaves and had other slaves who were born in my house. I also owned more herds and flocks than anyone in Jerusalem before me. I amassed silver and gold for myself, and the treasure of kings and provinces. I acquired male and female singers, and a harem as well—the delights of a man's heart. . . . I denied myself nothing my eyes desired; I refused my heart no pleasure. (Ecclesiastes 2:4-8, 10)

The king was wealthy and powerful, and he enjoyed the perks that accompanied his position. Marshaling his resources, Solomon ate and drank, planted and built, sang with his friends and slept with his harem.

In Ecclesiastes Solomon approaches pleasure like a scientist conducting an experiment.

> I said to myself, "Come now, I will test you with pleasure to find out what is good." But that also proved to be meaningless. "Laughter," I said, "is madness. And what does pleasure accomplish?" I tried cheering myself with wine, and embracing folly—my mind still guiding me with wisdom. I wanted to see

what was good for people to do under the heavens during the
few days of their lives. (Ecclesiastes 2:1-3)

It's fascinating to ponder Solomon's experiment. He doesn't say he
tested pleasure. Instead, he tested *himself* using pleasure. Pleasure
was just the Bunsen burner; it was his heart tested by the heat. And
what a blaze he lit!

Through Solomon's pleasure test—and our own—we learn that
we are a people of insatiable appetites. Solomon experimented in
the extreme. Remember his seven hundred wives and three hundred
concubines? While not to that extent, most of us have experimented
with a little hedonism. We turn on Netflix to watch one episode then
go to bed after ingesting an entire season, or we eat three bites then
inhale the whole bag. But how do we feel afterward? The promise
of pleasure never delivers. These experiments leave us overfull but
feeling empty.

Pursuing pleasure is a trap. We give ourselves pleasure, then
we're "given over" to it. Thinking we're the master, we freely indulge. But next thing we know, we're enslaved. Solomon wrote,
"Everyone's toil is for their mouth, yet their appetite is never satisfied"
(Ecclesiastes 6:7).

Whether the appetite is for food, sex, alcohol, or some other thrill,
we become paradoxically hungrier when we indulge. We stretch our
"stomachs," creating even more space to fill. After some time, "we're
not able to take joy in more modest rewards," Anna Lembke, doctor
and author of *Dopamine Nation* says. "Now, our drug of choice
doesn't even get us high. It just makes us feel normal. And when
we're not using, we're experiencing the universal symptoms of with-
drawal from any addictive substance, which are anxiety, irritability,
insomnia, dysphoria and craving."[13]

Pleasure-seeking may be driven by a desire to experience enjoyment or a desire to dull discomfort. But in either case, we aim to fill our hunger for God with a poor substitute, making an idol of pleasure and pulling us off mission as we chase this lesser good to our distraction and detriment.

Chasing pleasure becomes, in the words of social scientist Arthur Brooks, "addictive and animal" rather than "elective and human."[14] We find, as Solomon did, that few earthly pleasures can satisfy and none can satiate. "The eye never has enough of seeing, nor the ear its fill of hearing," Solomon wrote (Ecclesiastes 1:8).

Solomon doesn't sugarcoat his exploit, claiming, "Sure, I made some mistakes, but what a ride! I wouldn't change a thing!" He is a wiser and more honest guide: "I denied myself nothing my eyes desired; I refused my heart no pleasure. . . . When I surveyed all that my hands had done and what I had toiled to achieve, everything was meaningless" (Ecclesiastes 2:10-11). Pleasure is *hevel*, a fleeting vapor that quickly evaporates.

What was true for Solomon is true for us: The pursuit of pleasure always leaves us longing for more.

We live in a world saturated with pleasures. Good pleasures. Green grass, blues skies, and warm sunshine. A hard run, a good joke, and the smell of frying bacon. Clean sheets. Hearing Mozart in a concert hall, U2 in a stadium, and a daughter's delighted giggles at Disneyland. There's something good and right about all of it. Simple, sensory pleasures.

But how many leaders have lost their way because of the pursuit of pleasure? How many sought a thrilling experience but ended up with remorse and regret?

Some pursuits of pleasure are clearly outside the boundaries God has lovingly established. Other pleasures become problematic when

our loves are wrongly ordered and our love for pleasure begins to
distract or detract from our pursuit of God and the mission to which
he has called us. But there's sufficient evidence in Scripture to conclude that God is not antipleasure. In fact, our ability to experience
pleasure was created by God.

Our inability to be satisfied with under-the-sun pleasure is not
meant to intensify our pursuit of it—as though a higher dose of the
wrong medicine will cure us—but rather to point us above the sun.
This malfunctioning pleasure center of ours, it's a gift. It's a grace.
If we were satiable apart from God, would we ever seek him? If this
present kingdom were magical, would we pin our hopes on the one
to come? Maybe that is part of the ultimate gift that Solomon gives
us. He went all in with life's pursuits and pleasures and leads us to
the conclusion that this is not the path to satisfaction, purpose, or
missional living.

PLEASURE IS A FAULTY PURPOSE

To illustrate the age-old truth that there is no purpose in pursuing
pleasure, the Midrash—ancient Jewish commentary on the Hebrew
Scriptures—includes a story of a fox waylaid in his mission.

A fox happens upon a beautiful vineyard, but he cannot enter.
It is walled in on all sides. Then he discovers a very small hole,
but it is too small to pass through. So, being a shrewd fox, he
fasts for three days and then, lean and weak, slips in.

He proceeds to feast on all the food before him. But when
he tries to leave, again he cannot fit through the opening. So
he fasts for three more days and then, lean and weak, wriggles
his way home.

Turning to the vineyard, the fox says, "O vineyard, O
vineyard, how good are you and your fruits inside! I can't say

anything against the vineyard. It's good. All that is inside is beautiful and commendable. But what enjoyment has one from you? As one enters you, so he leaves."[15]

The paradox of pleasure is that it's both ever-present and ever-fleeting. The very moment we seem to have it in our grip, it's slipping through our fingers.

What's clear from our Scriptures, Solomon's experiment, and even modern science is that there's no point chasing pleasure. For Tony, for Solomon, and for us, it becomes a destructive life purpose. Those most doggedly determined to pursue happiness are those most likely to find it evades them.

Daniel Gilbert, one of the top researchers on happiness, studied the happiness of two groups of people: lottery winners and paraplegics. Surprisingly, there was no difference between the happiness of the two groups. Yes, initially winning the lottery came with a rush of raw pleasure, and initially sustaining the life-altering injury unleashed a deluge of despair, but everything gradually moved back to pre-life-changing-event levels. Just a few months on, the vast majority of people were no happier or sadder than they were before. Well, except for the lottery winners. A significant number of them ended up *less happy*.

Gilbert says:

> From field studies to laboratory studies, we see that winning or losing an election, gaining or losing a romantic partner, getting or not getting a promotion, passing or not passing a college test, on and on, have far less impact, less intensity and much less duration than people expect them to have. A recent study . . . showing how major life traumas affect people suggests that if it happened over three months ago,

with only a few exceptions, it has no impact whatsoever on your happiness.[16]

In a world full of shiny, desirable things, many would advise us to follow our hearts in pursuit of happiness. That advice comes straight from Ecclesiastes, where Solomon wrote, "Follow the ways of your heart and whatever your eyes see." But that wasn't the end of Solomon's sentence, even though it concludes the modern sentiment. Solomon went on to say, "But know that for all these things God will bring you into judgment" (Ecclesiastes 11:9).

Taken together, Solomon's words read more like a dare than wise counsel. Our under-the-sun pursuits are subject to above-the-sun scrutiny. And in that light, we can see that following our heart is a tricky way to walk.

On the one hand, we don't want to fall into rigid asceticism, as if rejecting life's good things is itself good. But on the other hand, we don't want to fall into carnal self-gratification, which, in the end, makes our desires uppermost and miscasts good things as ultimate goods.

Pleasure is not a pursuit but a gift. It's not what permeates our days but what punctuates them, pointing us back toward God and the invitation to find pleasure in our relationship with him. George Müller was a nineteenth-century hero of the faith, working with orphans in England. In his autobiography he shares an insight that reframed his pursuit of pleasure:

> I saw more clearly than ever that the first great and primary business to which I ought to attend every day was, to have my soul happy in the Lord. The first thing to be concerned about was not how much I might serve the Lord, how I might glorify the Lord; but how I might get my soul into a happy state, and how my inner man might be nourished.[17]

Get my soul happy in the Lord. Now that is the right destination for our pursuit of pleasure. How might our days be different if they started with our soul happy in the Lord? Might that help us live on mission?

Solomon pursued every pleasure on this horizontal plane and came up empty. But his father, David, went vertical. Despite his missteps, David was known as a man after God's own heart. Recognizing the emptiness of things under the sun, he sought pleasure in God and wound up full. Describing the opposite of his son's *hevelish* pursuits, David said, "You make known to me the path of life; you will fill me with joy in your presence, with eternal pleasures at your right hand" (Psalm 16:11).

DON'T FORGET TO REMEMBER

In 2 Timothy 3:4, Paul writes that people will be "lovers of pleasure rather than lovers of God." The course correction is ironically found in both fasting and feasting.

Knowing the propensity to make a good thing an ultimate thing, Scripture points us toward fasting. Jesus presumed it would be a regular practice among his followers (Matthew 6:16), and in the early church it was a vital discipline. The *Didache*, an early Christian teaching document generally dated to the late first century, says this: "Fast on the fourth [day] (Wednesday) and day of preparation (Friday)."[18]

Fasting brings limits. Our temporary self-denial not only makes space for prayer—reminding us that God alone can satisfy each time we feel a pang of longing—but also teaches us to flex our "no muscle." It's as if saying no to food, TV, or some other pleasure for a season allows us to say no to other temptations. Saint Athanasius the Great is said to have taught that "fasting possesses great power and it works glorious things. To fast is to banquet with angels."[19]

As spiritual disciplines, fasting and feasting share a common motivation: to point our eyes above the sun.

On the surface, feasting may sound like hedonism or gluttony, but Old Testament law prescribed seven major feasts that God's people were to observe each year (Leviticus 23). Additional feasts celebrated good things and significant milestones.

All of Israel's feasts, memorials, and celebrations were designed to help them remember their story. To recall the miraculous rescue God provided and the purpose he laid out for their lives. Feasting with God-honoring intentionality doesn't ask us to forgo pleasure; it points us back to the source.

Properly practiced, feasting amounts to celebrating how God has faithfully provided. Feasting reminds us to "taste and see that the Lord is good" (Psalm 34:8).

My colleague Dan Williams and his wife, Ashley, remember God's goodness each summer with an annual Steaksgiving feast. Steaksgiving commemorates the evening in 2012 when Dan was driving his dirt bike home from HOPE's office in Haiti and collided with a cow on the road. The outcome was grisly—for both Dan and the cow. Thrown from his bike, Dan landed in a drainage ditch beside the road. His left arm was bent ninety degrees in the wrong direction, with bones protruding through his skin, and he'd also fractured his right foot and dislocated his coccyx.

Dan was in tremendous pain and severely injured, but the nearest clinic could offer only some gauze and a cardboard splint. When staff explained that he would be transferred to a nearby hospital—where his sore throat had once been misdiagnosed as tonsillitis despite the surgical removal of his tonsils many years prior—Dan came undone. He had been serving in Haiti, but now he was sidelined by a senseless accident, and his prospects of a smooth recovery seemed dim. "God, where are you?" he cried out.

The answer came quickly. Friends arranged his transfer to a hospital in northern Haiti, where he was told there would be a doctor waiting. When he arrived, he was greeted by six physicians on a short-term medical mission to Haiti, including a general surgeon and an anesthesiologist. Though the X-ray machine was locked and its operator unreachable in a remote Haitian village, God miraculously provided a key, and the surgeon was able to view the break and set the bone, preparing Dan for a medical evacuation and more extensive surgery the next morning. Dan spent three months in recovery before returning to Haiti, providing ample time to ask, "Where was God in this?" and to conclude, "He was with me."

Every year, Dan and Ashley celebrate Steaksgiving to remember the cow and the clear way that they saw God do the miraculous. They invite friends, grill steaks, and feast, not holding back because this is a moment to celebrate how God was, and is, and will be with them. It's a purpose-filled feast that points partygoers' gaze above the sun.[20]

As we affirm God's goodness and celebrate his blessings through a feast, our hearts are inclined upward just like Dan and Ashley experience each Steaksgiving. I love the way a prayer of benediction in *Every Moment Holy* characterizes feasting as an act of truth telling, combating the enemy's lies that God is not good and desires to deprive us. "May this our feast fall like a great hammer blow . . . shattering the gloom, reawakening our hearts, stirring our imaginations, focusing our vision on the kingdom of heaven that is to come, on the kingdom that is promised, on the kingdom that is already, indeed, among us."[21]

Feasting helps us remember the larger story and points us onward in our mission to live and love well.

PRAYER

You are the true King, Father, and Friend.

Teach me to drive your truth into my inmost being.

Save me from the lies I tell myself.

I convince myself that pleasure can be found apart from you.

Help me to find my soul's satisfaction in you wholly:

    body, mind, spirit, soul

    all aligned in pursuit of you.

Let me surrender my goals, ambitions, motives,

    and pleasure-seeking all to the refining fire of your glory.

And may I emerge pure in heart, generous in spirit, aligned

    with heaven.

Only you, only you, can do this as I surrender to your kind

    and holy grace.

I love you Lord, my Savior.

—Ryan Skoog

FINDING OUR WAY—
RHYTHMS OF FASTING AND FEASTING

PLAN FOR FASTING		
Ideas	**Consider**	**My plan**
□ **Plan in advance:** Set aside a specific time to fast, for example from sunup to sundown. Write it on your calendar. Consider what you will fast. Some ideas include food, email, social media, complaining, or speaking.	**When will I fast? What will I fast?**	
□ **Do it together:** If possible, invite others to fast with you in community.	**Who will I invite to join me in my fast?**	
□ **Give yourself to prayer:** In all or a portion of the time you'd normally spend in the behavior from which you're abstaining, dedicate yourself to prayer. Let your pangs of desire point you toward God's presence.	**How will I incorporate prayer into my fast?**	
□ **Choose a theme verse for the fast:** In moments of discomfort, recite a memory verse or mission verse. Remind yourself of the *why* behind your fast with truth from Scripture.	**Which Scripture will guide my fast?**	

PLAN FOR FEASTING

Ideas	Consider	My plan
☐ **Create a theme:** As you enter a rhythm of feasting, consider a central theme like gratitude, growth, joy, wonder, or curiosity. Invite others to share their perspectives around the table as you discuss the theme.	**What ideas, memories, or Scriptures will serve as a theme for my feast(s)?**	
☐ **Make it memorable:** Go big and invite friends and neighbors. Decorate. As you recognize the abundance of God's blessing, share the abundance with others. Practice generosity and hospitality as you create a feast worth remembering.	**How will I create a memorable experience for my guests?**	
☐ **Bring the fun:** Consider sharing stories, games, or activities unique to your feast. What will you and guests remember about your time together?	**What can I do to make the feast fun?**	
☐ **An all-hands event:** Choose to involve your family and friends in the preparations and excitement leading up to the feast. Invite children to create invitations or decorations, ask friends to join in the theme by bringing unique dishes or games.	**Who will I invite to join? How will I involve them ahead of feast day?**	
☐ **Celebrate God's goodness:** Incorporate thanksgiving and celebration throughout the feast. Recount stories of God's faithfulness. Highlight lessons God has been teaching you and create an atmosphere of encouragement.	**Where will I incorporate worship and celebration?**	

6

THE PROBLEM WITH POWER

The strongest poison ever known
Came from Caesar's laurel crown.

WILLIAM BLAKE

A man who knew a thing or two about power once wrote, "Power tends to corrupt, and absolute power corrupts absolutely."[1] But Lord Acton's astute warning hasn't kept us from pursuing greater power, to the detriment of our mission.

In 1979, K. P. founded a nonprofit that championed the role of "native missionaries" in missions. He argued persuasively and compellingly for the pivotal role of same-culture and near-culture missionaries, raising funds to train more than one hundred thousand people to preach the gospel and plant and pastor churches in Southeast Asia, where many still live without the hope of the gospel.[2] It looked like a tremendous success, as the ministry raised millions and gained the backing of prominent pastors, but those inside the ministry saw another side.

Former staff paint a picture of a man swept up in the current of his own greatness, giving himself unearned accolades and honorifics, elevating himself above those he served or served alongside, wielding his authority to demand loyalty to his directives, and promoting a culture of unquestioning obedience. Ministry staff allege they were routinely instructed *not* to pray over directives they received from K. P.—including significant life changes like moving to another country—as that would constitute "independent passive rebellious nature."[3] One former team member recalled, "K. P. once said at a prayer meeting that it would be sin to say 'I'll pray about it' instead of 'Yes sir,' were he to request you move to Burma."[4]

K. P. and his upper echelon of ministry leaders believed *they*, rather than the individual pursuing God's leading, should be given the chance to fast and pray over staff members' decisions and direction.

"Staff was given the mindset that they may not fully know God's direction in their lives and were encouraged to ask leadership to do things, such as buy a house or a car or date a certain person, etc.," recounted one former staff member.[5] Another former employee lamented, "Questioning [ministry directives] is in no way tantamount to questioning God, but somehow it has become one and the same."[6]

Ministry leaders were asked to take a vow of loyalty—not to God or the church but to K. P. He led them in the following oath:

K. P.: Will you promise to submit to my leadership, my successors, and authorities of the church and the ministry set over you all the days of your life and ministry?

Respondent: I firmly make this pledge and promise in the name of God and before this congregation that I will submit and always remain loyal and faithful to your leadership and to your successors and in all matters.[7]

With K. P. decked out in robes, hat, and jewelry and decorated with the title "His Eminence Most Reverend Dr., Metropolitan Bishop," video showed staff and leaders in a ministry location kneeling or bowing before him, kissing his ring. One former staff member recalled a woman in an airport kneeling at his feet, grabbing his ankles, and bowing to him worshipfully. K. P. allowed it, brushing it off as a cultural practice that he needed to permit.[8] Staff who questioned K. P.'s approach to leadership were told they were privileged to be a part of the work God was doing in Asia.[9] That logic was used to excuse spiritual abuse.

While encouraging submission among his staff, K. P. himself had little accountability. His board included both his wife and son along with a handful of other members who had limited visibility into day-to-day operations.[10] When accusations against K. P.'s leadership became too loud to ignore, the board appointed one of its own long-standing members to investigate. This board member found the allegations of abuse of leadership credible, then saw how K. P.'s wrath turned against him when he presented his findings. "Your response was and still is a 'scorched-earth' approach that is willing to burn down anyone and anything in the way of your own conclusions and status," the board member told K. P.[11]

More than thirty former employees have spoken out. How many more kept quiet, believing their own mistreatment was a means to the end of spreading the gospel?

MISUSING POWER

I wonder if the slaves Solomon conscripted to build God's temple ever labored under the same delusion. Completing the temple was one of Solomon's most famed accomplishments. The project spanned seven years of his reign. The book of 1 Kings describes the grandeur of the structure, but it also describes the means Solomon employed to that end (1 Kings 5:13-16, 9:15).

Solomon's slaves were descendants of the captives from nations Israel had conquered (1 Kings 9:20). Under Solomon's leadership, Israel—who was marked by the legacy of Egypt's oppression— oppressed the nations of the world whom God had called them to bless (Genesis 22:18). The author of 1 Kings directs our attention to this blatant departure from God's way, tying the timeline of the temple to the timeline of Israel's emancipation: construction of the temple began "480 years after the people of Israel were rescued from their slavery in the land of Egypt" (1 Kings 6:1 NLT).

Through the prophet Micah, we are reminded "to do justly, to love mercy, and to walk humbly with [our] God" (Micah 6:8 NKJV). Solomon went zero for three on these core commands. He misused power as he built the temple, drifting from his mission—his higher calling—of following God and blessing the nations of the earth. Solomon's subjects, who were described as happy, safe, and well supplied (1 Kings 4:20, 25) early in his reign, came to know him as a leader who imposed "harsh labor and [a] heavy yoke" (1 Kings 12:4).

"By the time he dies, Solomon resembles Pharoah, the king of Egypt, more than he does his father David," the Bible Project summarizes.[12] Just as God opposed Pharoah, he opposed Solomon's abuse of power. Subjugating others may be one way to build an empire—or an organization—but it's not the way we advance God's kingdom.

The answer is not to disavow power, as though God calls us instead to impotence. Power is not evil, just as achievement, wealth, and pleasure are not evil. Andy Crouch writes that power is "a gift—the gift of a Giver who is the supreme model of power used to bless and serve." Crouch continues, "Power is not the opposite of servanthood. Rather, servanthood, ensuring the flourishing of others, is the very purpose of power."[13]

LISTEN, LEARN, AND LOVE

Cynt Marshall, former Dallas Mavericks' CEO and the first Black female CEO in the NBA, has frequently been recognized as one of the "50 Most Powerful Women in Corporate America,"[14] but she wields the tool of power very differently than K. P. and Solomon. "In my forty-plus years of work, I've learned that to be a good leader, I need to spend at least half of my working hours investing in the people around me: listening, learning, and loving them," she writes.[15]

In her years with Pacific Telephone and Telegraph, that approach led her to pole-climbing school, though no pole climbing was required of district managers. At the Mavericks, it meant she spent her first ninety days on the job meeting with employees at every level of the organization. First she'd ask about them, then she'd inquire where they saw themselves in five years, both personally and professionally. "I really believe my job as a leader . . . is to help you get there," she said.[16]

Bill Bright, evangelist and founder of Campus Crusade for Christ (now Cru), also led by serving. When Bright passed away in 2003, colleagues and friends shared beautiful tributes of his life and leadership. One retold a story of Bright's trip to South Korea in the early 1960s to receive an honorary doctorate, which doubled as a time to connect with thirty local staff members. Gathering at a nearby Christian conference center, staff left their shoes in the hall overnight, as is customary in Korea. Early in the morning, one conference attendee saw Bright polishing the shoes. After watching for some time, he inquired, "May I ask what you're doing?"

"I was hoping that no one would see me, except for perhaps the Lord," Bright deflected. "But I am so overwhelmed with the quality and the dedication of these Korean staff friends that I just wanted to do something to express my appreciation."[17]

Numerous studies have proven the benefits of servant leadership for employees, boosting work engagement, psychological safety, and morale. But servanthood isn't just a means to others' flourishing. It's the very key to our own. Our hearts need it.

WASH FEET AND WASH DISHES

When people think of life in a monastery, most think of the work of prayer and study. But according to Saint Benedict, manual labor is a third essential component of a monk's daily routine.

At the time of Saint Benedict, the prevailing attitude of the upper class was that physical work was degrading. The wealthy wouldn't deign to scrub a floor or develop calluses from chopping wood. However, the Benedictines believed that hard work is dignifying. Their community was marked by *Ora* (prayer), *Labora* (work), and *Lectio* (biblical study).

Those following the example of Benedict still divide their day into these three essential activities.

A close study of his timetable indicates that about three hours were spent in church at the Divine Office; five hours were devoted to manual labor; and two or three hours were given over to biblical study. According to the seasons of the year, both natural and liturgical, this schedule was fine-tuned, but it is fixed in its three-part form.[18]

Manual work was an essential part of their daily devotions. It wasn't just what the work accomplished in the monks' community but what it accomplished in their souls. It's difficult to be haughty while emptying a latrine.

They were simply following in the example of Jesus who washed feet and invited us to do likewise (John 13:14). Jesus always used his power and authority to love others and is described as one who "made himself nothing by taking the very nature of a servant" (Philippians 2:7).

As Andrew Murray wrote, "No place will be too low, and no stooping too deep, and no service too mean or too long continued, if we may but share and prove the fellowship with Him who spake, 'I am among you as he that serveth'" (Luke 22:27).[19]

In most cultures, footwashing no longer feels culturally relevant. But every culture has jobs that are not highly esteemed. Maybe it's emptying trash, cleaning toilets, or wiping tables. To "go and do likewise" is to let go of some element of privilege and prestige and follow our Servant King.

When power is amassed and accumulated, it inevitably causes leaders to lose their way. Unchecked power is the fast lane to a life off mission. Those who seem most likely to steward power and influence well are those who seem most eager to give it away. In light of the allure of power, leaders would be wise to employ simple guardrails.

When facing criticism, consider the response of "thank you" instead of a rush toward defensiveness.

When receiving accolades, consider how quickly you can point to others who helped along the way.

When you wonder if the pursuit of power and influence might be growing in your heart, actively invite others to take the stage while you cheer loudly from the audience.

When facing the temptation for a haughty heart, consider cleaning the latrines.

We serve a God who became a humble servant, so let's strive to go and do likewise.

PRAYER

Christ my friend and fortress,
    lead me to the secret place of trusting you in all things.
May I learn to run to you first, instead of my own devices.
Teach me to trust in your loving hands,
    instead of the work of my own.
Teach me to lean on your gracious strength,
    instead of leaning into my own.
Teach me to wait for your wisdom,
    before I move forward on my own.
And when I have reached the end of myself,
    help me lock eyes with you when my heart is afraid.
Lord, I believe, and at the same time help my unbelief.
Lord, I trust you, and at the same time help me trust.
When the waves rise and I feel alone, Father be near me.
When fears surround me on all sides, Jesus surround me.
When storms rage, Holy Spirit shelter me.
Help me let go of what I think I control
    and simply trust, simply believe.
No matter what I see, no matter what I feel,
    you love me
    and always will
    my Savior, my God.

—Ryan Skoog

FINDING OUR WAY—PRACTICING SERVICE

One of Jesus' most profound demonstrations of servant leadership was undoubtedly his act of washing the disciples' feet: a menial, unenviable task.

Reflect on the events of the past week. What basic tasks in your workplace, home, or church often go unnoticed? Which perhaps feel "beneath you"? Chart a few that you remember from previous days:

SUN	MON	TUE	WED	THUR	FRI	SAT

Without seeking recognition, what footwashing-equivalent task might God be inviting you to undertake this week? Consider completing one of the tasks you named above in service to someone else.

FINDING OUR WAY— WHAT YOU HAVE AND WHO YOU KNOW

Beyond what we may think of as traditional "acts of service," we have the opportunity to use our abilities, influence, and possessions to benefit others, stewarding power to serve, not subjugate.

1. *What do you have?* Consider the influence, talents, connections, and resources God has entrusted to you in this season. List each one that comes to mind in the sections of the left-hand column.

2. *Who do you know?* Next, think of the individuals in your sphere of influence. Write their names on the lines in the sections of the right-hand column.

3. *Make the match.* How might you share your influence, talents, connections, and resources with the people in your circle? Draw lines from each of your resources in the left-hand column to one or more individuals in the right-hand column. Who can you serve with the things God has entrusted to you?

WHAT YOU HAVE   **WHO YOU KNOW**

TALENTS, SKILLS, ABILITIES   WORK

[ ]   [ ]
[ ]   [ ]
[ ]   [ ]
[ ]   [ ]

CONNECTIONS   CHURCH

[ ]   [ ]
[ ]   [ ]
[ ]   [ ]
[ ]   [ ]

RESOURCES   COMMUNITY

[ ]   [ ]
[ ]   [ ]
[ ]   [ ]
[ ]   [ ]

7

THE QUEST FOR CONTROL

Never be afraid to trust an unknown future to a known God.

CORRIE TEN BOOM

In March 2020, fear was spreading as fast as the pandemic as we faced massive disruptions in our global work and imagined worst-case scenarios for HOPE International. It seemed as though the entire nonprofit sector was preparing for an impending storm, hunkering down and bracing for impact. Strategic plans were tossed aside as organizations entered survival mode. Industry experts advised conserving capital, preserving our institutions, and retreating. Anything less would be seen as irresponsible leadership.

With so much spinning out of control, HOPE's leadership team resonated with calls to "hunker down." Yet, at the same time, we couldn't deny that this was a *global* crisis. In-country staff shared dire needs in the communities where we served, in contexts where safety nets were almost nonexistent. Hunkering down would mean cutting funding for small-business owners and support for church-based savings groups when they were needed most.

HOPE's executive team prayed and deliberated. Sometimes we spiraled, reading one depressing headline and dire prediction after the next, bemoaning the many factors outside our control. But in one virtual meeting several weeks into the pandemic, while discussing ways to revise our budget, our director of development, Erika Quaile, said, "I think we need to trust our donors."

Trust. The word stopped us mid spiral.

It wasn't just trusting the generous supporters whose commitment to investing in dreams in the world's underserved communities had enabled our budget to steadily grow. It was, more fundamentally, trusting in God, who had provided in every season. The pandemic and accompanying restrictions and economic shocks were outside our control, but God wasn't wringing his hands. What if we believed the words of 1 Thessalonians 5:24, "The one who calls you is faithful, and he will do it"? What if we doubled down on our mission instead of doubling down on our efforts to control all the outcomes?

This moment shifted the question from "How do we hunker down?" to "How do we use what we have on behalf of the vulnerable?" That question led to others. If our bank account never decreased during the pandemic, was that success or a sign we had played it too safe? If our institution fared better than those we serve, were we serving our mission or ourselves? Would a watching world see us responding with courageous love and faithful surrender or fearful retreat?

As we asked and answered different questions, we came to see that pursuing control was pulling us off mission.

LIVING IN AMBIGUITY

Leaders possess no power to perfectly predict the future, yet we often feel the pressure of preparing our teams and organizations for it. Desiring to lead faithfully, we're forced to confront a reality Carey Nieuwhof identified, that "there's a fine line between faith and irresponsibility, and at times it's almost impossible to see."[1] We want to trust, but our inability to know what's coming—and often our powerlessness to stop it—is enough to leave any leader scrambling for some shred of control.

In Ecclesiastes 9:11-12, Solomon reflected on the whims of "time and chance" that have remained true through the ages:

> I have seen something else under the sun:
>> The race is not to the swift
>>> or the battle to the strong,
>> nor does food come to the wise
>>> or wealth to the brilliant
>>> or favor to the learned;
>> but time and chance happen to them all.
> Moreover, no one knows when their hour will come:
>> As fish are caught in a cruel net,
>>> or birds are taken in a snare,
>> so people are trapped by evil times
>>> that fall unexpectedly upon them.

Any honest leader recognizes that our best-laid plans might be disrupted, that we are impacted—for better or for worse—by factors beyond our control and outside our influence. As a result, some become paralyzed by anxiety, opting to remain blissfully ignorant of the future, making no plans or preparations at all. Others, like Solomon, spring into action.

In his own methods and might, Solomon sought to control the outcomes for Israel. Though the Bible tells us Solomon's reign was marked by "peace on all his borders" (1 Kings 4:24 NLT), both 1 Kings and 2 Chronicles detail the formidable military he established. It was David, not Solomon, who fought many battles, but the father and son took entirely different approaches to national security. In 2 Samuel 8, David—after capturing a thousand chariots, seven thousand charioteers, and twenty thousand foot soldiers in battle—hamstrung all but a hundred of the horses, obeying a command God gave to Joshua (Joshua 11:6).

He also turned to God for military direction, asking, as documented in 2 Samuel 5:19, "Shall I go and attack the Philistines? Will you deliver them into my hands?" David saw God's role as deliverance and his role as obedience. "Some trust in chariots and some in horses," David wrote in Psalm 20:7, "but we trust in the name of the LORD our God."

Solomon understood that he was meant to rely on God and not his own self-sufficiency. Surely he had grown up hearing the stories of how God had parted the Red Sea for the Israelites to cross in safety, collapsing the waters on Pharaoh's great army and his mighty chariots. Surely he knew that the walls of Jericho crumbled not with a superior siege plan but with a nonsensical trumpet blow. Could he have made it through childhood without hearing about Gideon's army of thirty-two thousand whittled down to three hundred so that God would be glorified in the ensuing victory?

And if all of that felt like ancient history to Solomon, there was his own father, slaying a giant with a slingshot to ensure God's people would not return to the yoke of slavery. "It is not by sword or spear that the LORD saves," David proclaimed as he courageously strode toward Goliath (1 Samuel 17:47).

We know Solomon got the message, since he wrote in Proverbs 21:31 (NKJV), "The horse is prepared for the day of battle, but deliverance is of the Lord." But Solomon seems to have drifted in his trust and dependence on God. Instead of trusting "deliverance is of the Lord," Solomon bankrolled a pretty strong backup plan in case God didn't show up.

In opposition to God's direction, Solomon "gathered chariots and horsemen." At the time, chariots were considered advanced military technology, and Solomon "had 1,400 chariots and 12,000 horsemen, whom he stationed in the chariot cities and with the king in Jerusalem" (2 Chronicles 1:14 ESV). Solomon sought to ensure no other nation dared go up against Israel—and if they did, he would rely on his military, not his God.

In all his wisdom, Solomon couldn't understand and trust God's upside-down ways. As 1 Corinthians 1:27 puts it, "God chose the foolish things of the world to shame the wise; God chose the weak things of the world to shame the strong." Solomon said it himself in Ecclesiastes 11:5, "As you do not know the path of the wind, or how the body is formed in a mother's womb, so you cannot understand the work of God, the Maker of all things."

Most of us are far more like Solomon than David, hedging our bets and clinging to control when God calls us to trust. We suffer with our own versions of the illusion of control, arrogantly assuming that we can control all the circumstances of our lives—or fearfully attempting to—and living in a way that insinuates we do life on our own.

But inevitably something happens to remind us that we are not in control. As Solomon concluded in Ecclesiastes 9:1, "The righteous and the wise and what they do are in God's hands, but no one knows whether love or hate awaits them." We fail. We suffer loss.

Shepherding an organization or a family eventually brings us to our knees, shattering the illusion of self-sufficiency. However, losing control is not the same as losing our way.

DEALING WITH DISASTER

Many months ago, Jill and I had a conversation with Joni Eareckson Tada—founder of Joni and Friends, an outreach to thousands of families affected by disability around the world—that we haven't stopped thinking about. As we spoke, Joni, who became quadriplegic when a diving accident broke her neck at the age of seventeen, expressed her sincere *gratitude* for quadriplegia.[2]

She didn't feel that way initially. "It's tough being a teenager," she remembered. "It's even tougher when you're seventeen and face life in a wheelchair."[3] This was not the life she envisioned, and at a time when most of her peers were enjoying the illusion of invincibility, Joni was confronting the reality of lifelong limitations. She described three years of depression and suicidal despair following the accident, until finally she prayed "the most powerful prayer" of her life. It was a prayer of surrender: "God, if I can't die, show me how to live, please!"[4]

In circumstances beyond her control and outside her choosing, Joni experienced the goodness and the presence of God. When she surrendered control, she began to live the truth of a passage she'd learned in Sunday school, "*All things* work together for good to them that love God" (Romans 8:28 KJV, emphasis added). She's seen God bring good to others—Joni and Friends has touched more than 14 million lives so far[5]—but also to her. "Every moment is extraordinary for the needy Christian," she said.[6]

For Joni, disability is a constant reminder of need and a lack of control, but for most leaders this can be a challenge. Joni speaks of the built-in temptation for Christian leaders to rely on their own strength. "Usually they rise to Christian leadership because they're good leaders. That is such a built-in danger," she says. "They're the ones who really have to be on guard."

She looks to Solomon's father, King David, as an example of a leader who knew his need of God. "If the king of Israel, who had everything, could say in Psalm 40:17, 'I am poor and needy,' then shouldn't we all find some neediness in our life?"[7]

Over the past five decades that Joni has lived with a disability and chronic pain, she's had significant experience praying through circumstances beyond her control. She describes how her prayers acknowledge both her will and her ultimate surrender to God's control. When facing a need, she spends 20 percent of her time in prayer addressing the need itself—asking for deliverance or a change in her circumstances—and 80 percent asking God to grant her "courage in it, patience in it, endurance in it." Through prayer, she asks, "What can I learn about Christ from this? How will God reveal himself to me through this?"[8]

JUST LIKE JEHOSHAPHAT

Though Solomon seemed to place his trust in advanced military technology, God wasn't done working through methods that made little human sense and ensured the glory was his. Just as he had done in the days of Moses, Joshua, Gideon, and David, God miraculously intervened in the nation's security when Jehoshaphat, a few kings down the line from Solomon, sought him. Jehoshaphat had already seen defeat in battle when God wasn't in it (2 Chronicles 18), and this time he took a different approach. As nations came to wage war against Judah, Jehoshaphat addressed God:

"Power and might are in your hand, and no one can withstand you" (2 Chronicles 20:6).

Humbly, he prayed, "We do not know what to do, but our eyes are on you" (2 Chronicles 20:12). That's a powerful prayer and a powerful way to live. To trust even when we don't know what to do.

With God's assurance that he was on their side, Jehoshaphat and the people of Judah left to confront this superior military power. "As they set out, Jehoshaphat stood and said, 'Listen to me, Judah and people of Jerusalem! Have faith in the LORD your God and you will be upheld; have faith in his prophets and you will be successful'" (2 Chronicles 20:20).

What Jehoshaphat did next defied human wisdom and logical military formation: He appointed singers to lead his army "to sing to the LORD and to praise him for the splendor of his holiness . . . saying: 'Give thanks to the LORD, for his love endures forever'" (2 Chronicles 20:21). Praise and thanksgiving became their battle cry, and "as they began to sing and praise, the LORD set ambushes against the men of Ammon and Moab and Mount Seir who were invading Judah, and they were defeated" (v. 22). God reminded the nation of Judah who controlled the outcome.

God still works in logic-defying ways. It still doesn't make sense to me today, but as HOPE prayerfully decided to move toward missional fidelity and away from strategic control during the pandemic, we experienced unprecedented growth and impact. Instead of decreasing our budget, pausing programs, and shrinking our activities or footprint, we stepped forward. Because we were deemed an essential business in the places we served, we were able to help entrepreneurs navigate the anxiety and uncertainty of the season. Opening our hands in a posture of surrender opened doors to advance the gospel. God did above and beyond what we could have asked or imagined, and the credibility of our mission in the communities where we served was dramatically enhanced.

When we decided not to hunker down in a self-protective posture, we didn't know what the outcome would be, but we knew God was inviting us to acknowledge our lack of control and trust his calling to continue investing in the places where we served around the world.

Dave Blanchard, founder of Praxis, wrote,

> Most of us are told by our parents, friends, educational system, and society at large to shoot for reasonable goals, which most often lead us to de-risk our lives by accumulating power, prestige, and possessions that insulate us from vulnerability and permit us to live for ourselves alone. . . . Many of us can be tempted to withdraw to safety and control by simply choosing easy quests.[9]

In other words, we design lives and pursue callings that feel very much within our control at the cost of our mission. Failing to step out in faith, we forfeit the opportunity to see God intervene.

What could we step into if we stopped chasing control? How do we surrender control and pursue the quests God intends for us?

ROWING WITH TRUST

Control is a misguided pursuit. Pastor and author Sharon Hodde Miller writes,

> The truth is, every time we face the urge to control, we are presented with a choice: Will we trust God or ourselves? This question is at the heart of our faith. If faith is believing in what we cannot see, control is the opposite. It is choosing to

trust what we can see—namely, our own power, knowledge, and intentions.[10]

Faithfully following Jesus involves risk. Like Jehoshaphat and Joni, I am trying to practice the spiritual disciplines of praise and prayer to grow my trust when I'm tempted to pursue control.

Both prayer and praise refocus our eyes "above the sun," pushing back against the self-focus of fear and anxiety. Pastor Louie Giglio writes that even when much is beyond our control, we can still control our focus.

> Worship and worry cannot occupy the same space; they can't both fill our mouths at the same time. One always displaces the other. We can either speak doom and destruction, kicking our worry and stress into high gear. Or we recount the size and character of the Almighty, releasing our outcomes to Him and centering our thinking in His sovereign plans. God encourages us to put on the garment of praise when we feel entangled by the spirit of heaviness. He gives us songs in the night, anthems for the dark night of the soul where worry and stress and fear lurk about. . . . Sing into the face of the uncertainty about a sure and unchanging God. We have the ability to determine where we look and to whom we look.[11]

Praise reminds us of God's greatness. It declares who God is—faithful, good, masterful architect of all creation—speaking truth to anxiety or ego. When we praise God, we awaken awe. "Awe arises when we confront a phenomenon that, by virtue of its vastness, challenges our understanding of the world," explains Berkeley University's Greater Good Science Center.[12] I can't think of anything more awe-inspiring than the Creator of the universe. In fact, in Scripture "awe" is a word reserved almost exclusively for God and his power.

Go for a walk and look up at the stars. Or look down at the beautiful mysteries of a flower. Be reminded of the greatness of God.

Awe is good for us. It's been linked to neurophysiological shifts like decreased inflammation, diminished self-focus, increased pro-social relationality, greater social integration, and a heightened sense of meaning and purpose.[13] These would be significant and meaningful impacts in anyone's life, but it's easy to imagine how leaders in particular might benefit.

Praise is a natural response to awe. It could involve music, as it did for Jehoshaphat's army, but it could just as easily consist of declarations spoken rather than sung (Psalm 35:28). To praise God is to speak the truth of who he is.

Prayer and praise belong together, and together they push back the darkness of fear and anxiety and the delusions of arrogance. We pray because of God's praiseworthy greatness. We pray because he is more competent, capable, and good than we can imagine and because the control that we crave belongs to him. And science shows that prayer, too, is good for us, even beyond the benefits of similar secular practices.

A 2005 study in the *Journal of Behavioral Medicine* found spiritual meditation to be more calming than secular meditation. Participants were divided into groups and assigned to meditate using words of self-affirmation ("I am love") or words describing a higher power ("God is love"). Researchers found that the spiritual meditation group showed greater decreases in anxiety and stress, more positive mood, and increased pain tolerance after four weeks of meditating for twenty minutes a day.[14]

Associate professor, clinical health psychology director at the University of Colorado Denver, and researcher Amy Wachholtz says prayer "lets you put down your burden mentally for a bit and rest," lightening our psychological load in the same way that handing off a heavy backpack would lighten a physical load.[15]

While these studies point to the impact of prayer, Jill and I have also personally experienced a deeper level of prayer in our lives over the past several years, largely due to the influence of our friend Ryan Skoog. Ryan provided the prayers for this book and has modeled what a life of prayer looks like for leaders. While he runs a global nonprofit and several businesses, he prioritizes prayer. He has invited us on a journey to more actively and intentionally create cultures of prayer in the places we work and in our lives. And we've experienced the impact.

We are not in control, but through prayer we have direct access to the one who is. Amid uncertainty, when fear and anxiety weigh us down, Jesus' invitation awaits: "Come to me, all you who are weary and burdened, and I will give you rest" (Matthew 11:28).

Amid the uncertainty of the pandemic, we came to Christ. When we could not gather with our global colleagues, we joined together for virtual global prayer gatherings, interceding for our programs, our supporters, those we serve, and our broader world. Before the pandemic, our spiritual integration team had occasionally hosted similar structured gatherings. But during the pandemic, we invited every program office to take a turn. I often think of the gathering hosted by my colleagues in the Republic of Congo. After a brief introduction, they invited all of us to pray out loud, simultaneously, microphones unmuted. What erupted was a beautiful cacophony, a chorus of praises and prayers in many languages, offered to God. What appeared to be a total loss of control was, in fact, a time of beautiful surrender for our team.

In times of uncertainty, leaders lose their way by clinging to their competencies instead of clinging to Christ. Though we long for control, God invites us to remember that no matter what happens in this life, he is Emmanuel, God with us. We are not alone, so we have reason to take heart. With praise and prayer, we can take the next step into an unknown future with a known God.

PRAYER

Hide me, oh Lord, in the shadow of your wings.
Help me dwell in the secret place of your presence,
    far from the lies, fears, temptations, and weary thoughts.
Protect my heart from straying,
    my mind from wandering,
    my soul from eroding.
Guard my soul
    from despair in the morning,
    from anxieties at night,
    from worries throughout the day.
I need your angels to lift me up
    so I don't trip on my own pride and self-reliance.
Strengthen my heart to resist the ways of this world
    and the little compromises that result in big failures.
I need you more than I could ever know, Father.
Remind me to hide in you, remind me to run to you
    throughout the day.
Today, I run under your wings, protected by your
    compassion and grace.
There is no safer place than you, Holy Friend, Holy God.

—Ryan Skoog

FINDING OUR WAY—
SURRENDERING CONTROL

Use the prayer guide to offer your plans and your anxieties to God in a posture of surrender.

Begin: Find a quiet place to reflect. Invite the Holy Spirit to meet with you and bring to mind areas of your life in which you may be clinging to control rather than being open to the Holy Spirit's leading.

Awe: Remind yourself who God is. Where do you notice Christ in creation? Look around at nature or up to the sky to see glimpses of the world God has made. Acknowledge ways that you are finite and God is infinite. List the imagery or attributes that come to mind:

Account: With God, name things you're prioritizing in this season and worries you may be carrying.

Plans and priorities:

Worries:

Offer: Read Philippians 4:6: "Do not be anxious about anything, but in every situation, by prayer and petition, with thanksgiving, present your requests to God." Visualize yourself removing each anxiety from a backpack you carry and handing it to Jesus. Repeat a simple prayer of thanksgiving like, "Thank you for carrying my burdens."

Close: With palms up, sit quietly and consider what words or truths the Holy Spirit brings to mind. Jot them down.

Commit: Commit to regularly offering your plans and your anxieties to God. Write a note on your calendar, phone, or desk where you will be frequently prompted toward trust rather than control.

PART THREE

STRONG CURRENTS

8

THE NEED FOR SPEED

There's a price to pay for the speed,
and that is danger.

ELLEN MACARTHUR

Jason's dream of raising awareness of a global atrocity came true. An activist filmmaker, Jason and his colleagues successfully leveraged the power of YouTube and social media to shine a spotlight on atrocities committed thousands of miles away in Central Africa. They brought a faraway crisis into American living rooms, believing "the problem is 99% of the planet doesn't know" about atrocities committed by a rebel warlord who had abducted tens of thousands of children, enslaving them as soldiers and sex workers.[1] Their awareness-raising film went viral. Within twenty-four hours they had hit a million views. "We popped champagne," Jason remembers. "It's the only time we've ever celebrated."

He describes what came next as a "tsunami."[2]

Before, they had been excited when their organization made the local news. Now, interview requests were pouring in from the likes of CNN and Ryan Seacrest. "No one left the office," Jason says. Their sole public relations worker—a volunteer intern—couldn't get her inbox below four thousand new messages, no matter how quickly she responded. Jason's phone was getting "ten text messages every second." Within forty-eight hours, he did seventeen interviews and squeezed in a sleepless red eye from Los Angeles to New York City.[3] He remembers the exhaustion and the growing number of detractors as well as fans that came with the exposure.

Within a week of the film's release, it had received one hundred million views, setting a YouTube record at the time. Stars such as Justin Bieber, Rihanna, Kim Kardashian, and Oprah Winfrey shared their platforms to spread the message.

And then Jason very publicly broke down, the weight of the stories he carried, the mission he championed, the criticisms he bore, and his frenzied pace overtaking him. It was heartbreaking. If I had been in Jason's shoes, getting all the attention I'd ever imagined for HOPE and the eradication of global poverty, I know that I would have kept a similar pace. Who would turn down an interview with CNN or a conversation with Bono? It was so easy to see how Jason's story could have been mine if I, like him, had gotten just what I wanted.

Reflecting on what happened, Jason says, "I should have been listening to my loved ones. . . . I should have slowed down, let go, and instead I chose to keep pushing and keep pushing. . . . That's something, of course, I'll have to live with my whole life."[4]

In the wake of the organization's meteoric rise came a precipitous fall, their budget plummeting from $16 million in 2012 to $1.7 million five years later. The nonprofit still exists, focusing on local programs in Central Africa. "Today, we are intently focused on supporting and expanding nimble, community-based solutions that are making children and families safer from violence in some of our world's most remote and isolated regions," they write.[5] They're rebuilding at a slower pace that affords time to scale and time to take a step back. Jason continues to dedicate himself to inspiring action through compelling storytelling.

THE PACE OF DRIFT

Carl Jung wrote, "Hurry is not of the devil; hurry is the devil."[6] Yet busyness is a hallmark of modern life. It's paraded in our culture as though a busy life is equivalent to a productive one. If you listen carefully, you'll hear the boast beneath people's busyness. A calendar full of commitments is like a Girl Scout's sash full of merit badges. It makes us feel important. *If we weren't so necessary, we wouldn't be stretched so thin.*

While technology once held the promise of a more reasonable pace—a four-day work week even—instead, we suffer from "digiphrenia," a word coined to describe how technology "encourages us to be in more than one place at the same time." I remember playing hide-and-seek with my children when they were younger and intentionally choosing the very best hiding spots so that I could sneak in a few more moments of work email, engaging in their game while remaining deeply disengaged. It's not working. In our effort not to miss anything, we often miss everything.

We rise early, log in, caffeinate, and multitask all day long. Sometime near the end of the cycle we feel exhausted, but our minds won't shut down. We know that this harried lifestyle has many consequences, but we don't have time to think about that now.

John Ortberg, author and former pastor of Menlo Park Presbyterian Church, famously asked philosopher Dallas Willard about the key to spiritual health. Willard said, "You must ruthlessly eliminate hurry from your life."

Ortberg humorously claims to have replied, "Check. Got it. What else?"

"There is nothing else," Willard responded. "You must ruthlessly eliminate hurry from your life."[7]

Hurry is not a virtue! In fact, the Bible associates it with all kinds of harm, particularly in the book of Proverbs (emphasis added below):

It is the wicked whose feet *rush* into evil (Proverbs 6:18).

They are *swift* to shed blood (Proverbs 1:16).

They are *quick* to quarrel (Proverbs 20:3).

They make *haste* and miss the way (Proverbs 19:2).

How many times do we miss the way in our haste? Hurry is a strong current causing us to miss the way.

MISSING WHAT MATTERS

When my friend Matt mentioned his recent thrill driving on a professional racetrack, I was eager to learn more. Using research for this book as a convenient excuse, I asked if he could share what he observed during his fast and furious driving adventure. To my delight, Matt invited me to experience my own thrills, joining him for a ride in his BMW M8 Carbon Fiber Competition Model.

We didn't just talk; in a safe location, we experimented with acceleration and speed. Six hundred and forty horsepower were fully employed in what I can only describe as our blastoff. I was able to experience g-force, horsepower, and speed far beyond the capabilities of our family's Honda.

It was difficult to form coherent questions in my exhilaration, but as we returned to a slower pace to process the experience, Matt told me that the faster he drove, the more limited his vision became. The more speed, the more he narrows his gaze and focuses only on what is right in front of him, missing what's around him. Driving in "sport mode," even the display panel goes black to minimize distraction. Those who designed the car knew that the driver's full focus and attention needed to be limited when traveling at high speeds.

With speed comes limited vision.

There is something thrilling about speed, but we all know the very real consequences of living too fast. We can't see anything beyond what we're working on. We can't consider anything beyond the immediate future. We can't focus on the people right next to us, and at some point, we start to lose control. When it happens, it's a race to find the brake before real harm ensues.

On the road and in life, high-speed pursuits harm not only the driver but also others in proximity. As Alan Fadling, cofounder of Unhurried Living, writes, "The hurried leader may sacrifice their well-being and the well-being of their team for the sake of productivity and efficiency."[8]

A HURRIED SOUL

Despite the wisdom Solomon shared in the book of Proverbs and his counsel against haste, from the beginning of his rule, he made decisions marred by a spirit of hurry. His father, David, longed to build a temple for the Lord and made extensive preparations for the building project, but God would not allow David to complete the work because he was a warrior who had "shed blood" (1 Chronicles 28:3). That privilege and responsibility passed to Solomon. With peace in the kingdom, Solomon had no need to shed blood, yet he, too, struggled to live as a man of peace when his earthly father charged him with the bloody task of settling old scores and dispatching with his enemies (1 Kings 2). There's no record of Solomon consulting his heavenly Father for wisdom on the matter.

Solomon also seems to have sped into the marriages that helped to lead him astray. Solomon was already married to an Ammonite woman named Naamah when he ascended to the throne. Her name meant "pleasant," and because she was Solomon's first bride, some speculate that Solomon's Song of Songs was written for her.[9]

But upon assuming the throne, one of Solomon's first royal acts was to marry Pharaoh's daughter. Following David's military conquests, Israel was seen as a rising power. Egypt, at the time, seemed to be waning in influence. "As a result, it may have been more willing to ally itself with Solomon," writes biblical scholar Philip Stern.[10]

Solomon's expedient marriage secured an alliance with Egypt, but perhaps even more than that, it sent a message to other nations that Solomon was a person of significance. Egypt was notoriously stingy with its brides. One fourteenth-century BC letter written by a Babylonian king to an Egyptian Pharaoh said, "When I wrote to you about marrying your daughter, in accordance with your practice of not giving (a daughter), you wrote to me, 'From time immemorial no daughter of the king of Egypt is given to anyone.'"[11]

In marrying an Egyptian princess, Solomon communicated his influence and significance to the nations of the ancient world, ensuring they, too, would eagerly ally with Israel. He seemed to know it wasn't right, as 2 Chronicles 8:11 (NLT) recounts how Solmon moved his new wife, Pharaoh's daughter, to a new palace, explaining, "My wife must not live in King David's palace, for the Ark of the LORD has been there, and it is holy ground." Solomon's marriage covenant tarnished Israel's covenant with God.

Again we see the breadth of Solomon's gap between knowing and doing. Solomon went on to form marriage alliances with Moab,

Ammon, Edom, Sidon, and Hatti, "nations about which the LORD had told the Israelites, 'You must not intermarry with them, because they will surely turn your hearts after their gods'" (1 Kings 11:2). All told, he had seven hundred wives of royal birth, averaging one marriage every twenty-one days of his forty-year reign. Apparently, Israel was a land flowing with milk, honey, and wedding cake.

Solomon's polygamy wasn't honoring to his marriage vows, and it wasn't honoring to God. This wasn't God's way; it was a shortcut pursued in Solomon's haste to establish his own significance. Ultimately, Solomon paid a steep price, summarized in 1 Kings 11:3: "His wives led him astray."

Solomon's decisions reveal his willingness to shortcut and sidestep God's plan for his reign and for the nation of Israel. What sounded like an expedient path to cementing his own power sowed the seeds of his kingdom's dissolution. Later, in Ecclesiastes, this husband of many counseled, "Enjoy life with the wife whom you love . . . because that is your portion in life" (Ecclesiastes 9:9 ESV). When we rush, we lose our way. When we rush, we make foolish decisions, leading to regret and remorse.

Dallas Willard knew of what he spoke. A restless life wounds others and ruins oneself. In contrast, a restful life refreshes both others and ourselves.

Avoiding drift requires a change of pace. A time and place to regularly pause, consider, take stock. We won't know that we're veering off course until we can slow down enough to look up and check our location. In Ecclesiastes Solomon counsels us to "look" forty-seven times. To examine. To press into the actual facts of this fleeting life. The best way to avoid derailing our life is to look carefully.

SLOWING DOWN

A few years ago, my friend Greg and his wife took a bucket-list trip to Israel with another couple. Others who had made the trip cautioned, "Be selective. You can't see it all, so don't even try. Choose a limited number of sites and linger there. Take your Bibles. Be still. You can go back again sometime and get what you missed." Despite the counsel, they crammed as much into their nine days as possible, rejecting the spiritual retreat and opting for the whirlwind tour, leaving too few precious experiences. As Greg reflected on the trip, his highlight was the single moment when they slowed down by the Huldah Gates at the Temple Mount, where Pentecost broke out and the first three thousand new Christians were baptized. Few people see that spot, but Greg spent two hours there, much of it in quiet. With this slower pace, the significance of what he beheld could finally sink into his heart.

As someone eager to fit in as much as possible, I resonate with Greg's story. I've had my own whirlwind tours, only in retrospect realizing that I missed the heart of the experience. As an adrenaline junkie, I'm beginning to learn how to move at a slightly slower pace and make more purposeful decisions.

The philosopher Blaise Pascal spoke of it this way:

> I have often said that the sole cause of man's unhappiness is that he does not know how to stay quietly in his room. . . . What people want is not the easy peaceful life that allows us to think of our happy condition, nor the dangers of war, nor the burdens of office, but the agitation that takes our mind off of it and diverts us. That is why we prefer the hunt to the capture. That is why men are so fond of hustle and bustle; that is why

prison is such a fearful punishment; that is why the pleasures of solitude are so incomprehensible.[12]

The first word of Hebrew worship is "hear." "Hear, O Israel, the LORD our God, the LORD is one" (Deuteronomy 6:4). God's people live not by eating but by hearing. They live not by bread alone but by every word that comes out of God's mouth (Deuteronomy 8:3). Paul carries this into the New Testament, saying, "So faith comes from hearing, and hearing through the word of Christ" (Romans 10:17 ESV).

How well do we hear in a hurry?

Good listening is always associated with stillness. We must stop, turn down the background music, look into a person's face, and actively acknowledge that they're speaking to us. We can't fulfill our mission to love God and love others if we're not listening, and we can't listen in a hurry.

BREAKING THE ADDICTION

Most of us don't need to be convinced that we're addicted to hurry. We know it. We feel it. We confess we've been living from moment to moment, never fully in the moment, almost incapable of being fully present.

Douglas Rushkoff observes, "Our society has reoriented itself to the present moment. Everything is live, real time and always-on."[13] He calls it present shock and goes on to say that it's not just that we speed things up but that we diminish anything that isn't happening right now. It's no way to live, but it is a way to lose our way.

When the life of a leader is rushed, it's hard to see when and where we've gotten off course. Who has time to pause and look where we are heading when there is always more to do? We become so preoccupied with doing that we fail to pause and ask if the things we're doing are aligned with our mission.

So how might we find the gift of stillness?

Some people receive an unwelcome opportunity to reconsider the pace of life in the form of a crisis, a medical emergency, unemployment, or burnout that brings all the hurry to a halt. We're sidelined, and we think the jig is surely up. But then something amazing happens. We slow down and rest. We think. We deactivate the reactive amygdala and engage the "rational cortex" of the frontal lobe.

Priorities are reassessed, some habits change. We bring the RPMs back under the red line. Eventually we get back to work, but we do it in a different mode. We establish better boundaries and protect our time at home. The tension dissipates and we feel muscles slowly relax in our necks. We smile more.

Of course we don't need to pay such high tuition to learn these lessons. It doesn't require a layoff or a health scare. It is possible to make the changes now, of our own accord, before they're foisted upon us.

We can't find the solution until we understand the problem, so we must begin by diagnosing the root of our busyness. What drives us so much? Is our frenetic pace prompted by our discomfort with silence? Is it a mad dash for an idolatrous desire? Or maybe an attempt to prove ourselves to ourselves, our family, or to God?

EXHAUSTION IS EXPENSIVE

Some massive disasters have occurred in my lifetime, including the nuclear meltdowns at Three Mile Island and Chernobyl, the Challenger space shuttle explosion, and the Exxon Valdez oil spill. A common contributor in each of these—and many smaller-scale disasters—is exhaustion. Overly tired people delayed responses and made poor decisions. Fatigue has dire, sometimes deadly consequences.

How many of us have our own spills, crashes, and meltdowns looming? How much personal mission drift is caused by a pace of life that is harming our soul?

During a global financial crisis, my friend and colleague Ghena Russu experienced a personal crisis from exhaustion. Invest-Credit, the microfinance institution he leads in Moldova, saw a rapid rise of portfolio-at-risk, as families were slower to repay their loans. Donors and investors began to question the long-term viability of the program into which Ghena had poured so much of his life. Fearing for the institution's future, Ghena and his team worked tirelessly to resolve the problems.

They spent more time visiting clients, scrutinizing all aspects of their enterprise, and fastidiously measuring improvement. Powerless against a global financial crisis, nothing they did moved the needle. In fact, their problems seemed to grow, even as they worked harder.

As executive director of the organization, Ghena took the challenges personally. Working for weeks without a day off, his body began to protest. Unable to sleep or eat solid foods, he lost over twenty-five pounds in a month. Afflicted with severe headaches, more than once he had to pull his car off the road until they passed. Eventually, he spent four weeks in the hospital while doctors tried to diagnose his illness. In the end it was simple: too much hurry, too little rest.

During his hospital stay, with little to do but think, Ghena reacquainted himself with his priorities. He identified significant drift between his theology and his praxis. His forced sabbatical gave him time to dialogue with God about foundational work questions. Do I lead as though my identity is defined by this role? Do I lead as though the numbers at work measure my value as a person? Am I a failure if I can't save this institution from a global financial crisis?

"Staring at the hospital ceiling, I eventually came to my senses like a prodigal son," Ghena says. He came to see clearly that his former pace was not helping the organization—and it was killing him. Ghena acknowledged the need for course correction. He couldn't return to work and expect different results while observing the same practices that had permitted such significant personal drift. Humbly, he asked the Invest-Credit staff to forgive him for the unhealthy posture he had modeled as their leader.

To recalibrate, Ghena considered his values and evaluated his short-, mid-, and long-term goals to ensure his priorities aligned with those values. A mentor helped him recognize how worry and hurry were connected in his life and encouraged him to memorize Philippians 4:6-7, "Do not be anxious about anything, but in every situation, by prayer and petition, with thanksgiving, present your requests to God. And the peace of God, which transcends all understanding, will guard your hearts and your minds in Christ Jesus." Then he took the practical steps of reducing his hours, slowing his pace, forcing himself to take days off, and exercising more frequently.

In short, he took his first tentative steps toward sabbath keeping, a discipline that has grown in his life in the years since.[14]

SABBATH AS A GIFT

Scripture and courageous leaders who have broken their addiction to hurry show us that the path to living on mission lies well outside our frenzied pursuits. Sabbath keeping, a habit commended to us since the dawn of creation, may be just what we need to forestall the emptiness, or *hevel*, in our work.

The Hebrew word *sabbath* means "cessation." Suspension. Stop. God modeled it in creation, then reiterated its importance by making it one of the Ten Commandments: "Six days you shall labor and do all your work" (Exodus 20:9). This instruction was given to the Israelites just after their escape from slavery in Egypt. To people whose value had been directly connected to their production, this idea of resting from labor was an assertion of identity. It said their worth had nothing to do with their production and everything to do with who they were as the culmination of God's good creation. "Sabbath is a counternarrative to a culture of production and consumption," one reader of Old Testament scholar Walter Brueggemann summarized.[15] In our own culture of production and consumption, where we've largely bought into the lie that we are what we do, we still desperately need this counternarrative.

Christ's followers have, in the words of author A. J. Swoboda, "uncritically mimicked the rhythms of the industrial and success-obsessed West. . . . We have come to know Jesus only as the Lord of the harvest, forgetting he is the Lord of the Sabbath as well."[16] We drift so naturally toward busyness that rather than spending time with God, entering into relationship with him, we do things for him.

In contrast, Jesus' vision for how we live in God's kingdom is rooted in rest. It's not the type of rest that marketers try to sell us, in the form of timeshares, self-care routines, or premium bedsheets. But as author and founder of Practicing the Way, John Mark Comer, has observed, almost all advertising uses sabbath imagery. Marketers know we crave sabbath. Ironically, they're working overtime to sell us something Jesus already offers.[17]

One time some people came to Jesus and asked, "What must we do to do the works God requires?" And Jesus answered, "The work of God is this: to believe in the one he has sent" (John 6:28-29). The people wanted to do works plural. So typical. There must be a million things God requires of us! No, Jesus says. The singular work is this: believe in me. By most classifications that's not even work—that's just faith.

Jesus says in John 15:5 that abiding, not haste, is the path to fruitfulness in his kingdom: "If you remain in me and I in you, you will bear much fruit; apart from me you can do nothing." It's a picture not of striving but sabbath-resting in the Father's presence.

Sabbath teaches us something about who we are, and it also teaches us something about who God is. Pastor and author Adele Ahlberg Calhoun writes, "God's sabbath reality calls us to trust that the Creator can manage all that concerns us in this world as we settle into his rest."[18]

Sabbath is a great act of faith. In sabbath keeping, we leave money on the table. In sabbath keeping, we set aside our preoccupation with advancing our career or ticking every box on our to-do list. While many others are out killing it (or is that killing themselves?), we're away from our desks practicing rest that prompts worship.

Tomorrow we may arrive at work to find the world has passed us by, but that's the chance we'll have to take if we're serious about remaining true to our mission as followers of Christ. The odds are we'll hit the ground running happier and more focused as our new week begins. And over the course of many weeks, we'll be healthier and more refreshed than those who lack the faith to shut it down. We'll find this well-attested, God-commanded, counterintuitive practice serves us well.

Leadership mentor and minister Wayne Muller writes, "Our culture invariably supposes that action and accomplishment are better than rest, that doing something—anything—is better than doing nothing. Because of our desire to succeed . . . we do not rest." But here's where drift comes in.

> Because we do not rest, we lose our way. We miss the compass points that would show us where to go, we bypass the nourishment that would give us succor. We miss the quiet that would give us wisdom. We miss the joy and love born of effortless delight. Poisoned by this hypnotic belief that good things come only through unceasing determination and tireless effort, we can never truly rest.[19]

It might just be during a sabbath rest that we identify that we're going off course early enough to change direction and avoid considerable hurt and harm. Rest is required to reorient ourselves to our mission. Rest is an essential discipline if we seek to avoid losing our way.

SAYING NO SO THAT WE CAN SAY YES

Sabbath isn't an invitation to add one more thing to an already overfilled schedule. For most of us, saying yes to God's invitation (and command!) to rest means we will need to say no to something else to create that margin.

Warren Buffett famously wrote, "The difference between successful people and very successful people is that very successful people say 'no' to almost everything."[20] We probably won't have to take it that far, but the point is a good one. If we want to be "very successful" in matters of supreme importance, we simply cannot say yes to every invitation.

As I started to adjust my pace, I began waiting twenty-four hours before responding to any invitations that require travel. This buffer allows me to consider if it's truly a priority. Second, for every yes, there must be a corresponding no. What will I decline to compensate for this added responsibility? Something other than sabbath has to give. Managing our schedule is like managing our closet. For every new item we get, wisdom says we rid ourselves of an old one. Similarly, rather than overstuffing our calendar, understand that every yes must engender a no. It's the only way to maintain sanity, balance, and the practices of sabbath.

Carving out time for sabbath has refined my focus. It's required planning, delegation, and sometimes disappointing someone when they wish I'd say yes but I have to say no. It hasn't been easy, but it has been good. I've found that the contents of my not-to-do list have become every bit as important as my to-do list.

We need discipline, resolve, and a little imagination to protect margins to listen, love, pray, and rest. But we do not finish well when we are running ragged. So if you, like me, are tempted to pick up the pace, sabbath might just be the gift you need to receive.

PRAYER

Jesus,
Help me trade the race of this earth for the rhythm of heaven.
My restless heart once again needs to find its rest in you.
Teach me your light burden; teach me your easy yoke.
I give you the weight I feel, right now,
    the burdens weighing the core of my soul.
I place them into your strong hands.
Help me slow down, to remember, to receive, to rejoice.
Fill me with your love, so I may give your love to others.
Fill me with joy, to bring joy to others.
Fill me with peace, so I can give your peace to others.

May I receive your patience, so I can give your patience to others.

May I receive your kindness, so I can be kind to others.

May I receive your goodness, so I can be good to others.

Heal my past hurts; keep them from guiding me.

Calm my fears; keep them from leading me.

Remove my bitter feelings; keep them from staining my soul.

Too often I set out on your work, in my own way, in my
own strength.

I remember you are with me.

I remember your relentless morning mercy and endless
evening grace.

I remember the storehouses of heaven are available
throughout the day.

Help me find sabbath rest in you, kind Savior, my Lord and friend.

—*Ryan Skoog*

FINDING OUR WAY— A SABBATH FRAMEWORK

Use these suggestions to create your own rhythm of sabbath. Consider adapting the framework to *stop*, *rest*, *delight*, and *worship* as you aim to build an intentional day for spiritual renewal and connection with God.

- *Mark out* a twenty-four-hour time period for weekly sabbath.

- *Invite others* to sabbath alongside you. Make sabbath a family habit or consider inviting close friends in your community to participate with you in the same weekly rhythms.

- *Sabbath* is countercultural and a helpful way to stay on mission. It's more difficult to lose our way when we are well rested, spiritually healthy, focused, and regularly practicing sabbath. At first, practicing sabbath may feel uncomfortable.

Commit to move toward rest each week and no longer away from it.

- *Plan* for sabbath in advance. Traditionally, a preparation day has been required to make sure the sabbath is free from work. Create a list of shifts you will need to make in order to have a full twenty-four hours of worship and rest.

- *Consider* a digital detox in which you reduce or remove technology for a full twenty-four hours.

STOP Make space to rest by stopping.	
Disconnect	**Set boundaries to intentionally avoid work.** *Examples:* Refrain from working on projects, researching, and checking email, social media, or calendars. Try to avoid even discussing work or allowing your thoughts to linger on the work week ahead. Be present.
Decide	**Choose what non-work-related tasks to omit during your sabbath.** *Examples:* Some choose to avoid cleaning, yard work, paying bills, shopping, or other tasks to prepare for the week ahead.
REST Intentionally invest in rest to rejuvenate your whole person.	
Physical rest	**Set aside time for extra sleep.** If at all possible, sleep in! Don't set an alarm. Or choose to nap. Sleep is restorative for the mind and body. God designed our bodies to need it for a reason. Let your body and mind recover from the week.
Emotional rest	**Be intentional about where you focus on sabbath.** Consider a break from the news cycle and from social media.

DELIGHT
Refresh your soul with activities that spark joy, wonder, and gratitude.

Pleasure stack	Sabbath is a great way to savor the things you enjoy most. A fun way to find more enjoyment is by pleasure stacking multiple of your favorite things together on the sabbath. *Example:* Go for a hike with family or friends, stopping for your favorite dessert afterward.
Destination	Where in your neighborhood do you most often find joy? It could be a park, restaurant, friend's house, or overlook. Choose to go there often when you practice sabbath! Delight in your special places with the people you most enjoy.
Refreshment	Fill your sabbath with activities that truly refresh you. Maybe it's catching up with a friend on a walk. Perhaps you set aside time to engage in a hobby like woodworking, painting, or leisure reading. The goal is to find joy and refreshment in the activities you would normally be challenged to make time for throughout the rest of the week.

WORSHIP
Focus your heart on grateful praise and adoration of God.

Abide	Set aside time to abide in God's presence. This doesn't always need to be as formal as Bible reading or quiet devotion, although that may be included. Consider going on a prayer walk, practicing silence and solitude, creatively memorizing Scripture, journaling, or offering your thoughts to God in conversation.
Adore	Throughout the day, focus on attributes of God's character. Orient your heart toward gratitude, telling God of the things you notice in the world around you that bring you joy and delight. Find opportunities to thank him often. Notice his presence.
Contemplate	Spend time in a location that evokes awe and wonder of God. Maybe you feel God's peace when you spend time in nature. Maybe you see his beauty reflected in your children or a friend. Contemplate his creation and the gifts all around you.

9

THE ISLAND EFFECT

The Creator arranged things so that we need each other.

Basil of Caesarea

"I am committed to finishing well," Ravi once declared.[1] But unfortunately, he didn't.

Ravi was a prominent Christian apologist and evangelist who founded an international ministry that aimed to defend the Christian faith and spread the gospel. When he died of cancer in May 2020, there was an immediate outpouring of testimonies from those whose faith had been deepened by his teaching. But these accolades were closely followed by a slower-trickling series of allegations that revealed a dark side of his life and work, which had previously been alleged in part but excused by Ravi and those nearest him.

In one talk recorded a year before Ravi's death, he uttered a sentence that now rings ominously true: "Those of you who have seen me in public have no idea what I'm like in private." He went on to exhort listeners that God knows, "And I encourage you today to make that commitment and say, 'I'm going to be the man in private who will receive the divine accolade, "Well done, thou good and faithful servant."'"

What must Ravi have been thinking when he uttered those words, knowing the truth of his private life?

According to investigations by *Christianity Today* and an independent law firm posthumously hired by his ministry, Ravi abused scores of women over many years, both in the United States and abroad. He also lied about his academic credentials, exaggerated his accomplishments, and misused ministry funds to support his lavish lifestyle and predatory behavior.

The *Christianity Today* report did not mince words, describing the apologist as one who "leveraged his reputation . . . to abuse massage therapists in the United States and abroad over more than a decade while the ministry led by his family members and loyal allies failed to hold him accountable."[2] Ravi used his power, influence, and reputation to manipulate, exploit, and silence his victims, while maintaining a façade of integrity and holiness.

His downfall shocked and saddened many Christians who looked up to him as a role model and a champion of the faith. It also raised questions about the accountability, transparency, and culture of his ministry and other Christian organizations.

Because even those nearest Ravi seemed genuinely shocked by the truth of the allegations, I wondered if there were any real friendships. Did anyone ask Ravi the difficult questions when he started going off mission? Was there any evidence that people knew him and loved him enough to call him out for the compromises along the way?

I expected to find a man deeply isolated, perhaps by an overloaded schedule or frequent travel. Although most who met Ravi described him as humble, I silently speculated that perhaps he pridefully kept his distance, finding no equals with whom he could relate. But what I found instead was something that alarmed me still more: Ravi engaged in the type of friendship that I've always considered protective.

Upon Ravi's death, a fellow ministry leader recalled their weekly WhatsApp chats, "sharing the Scriptures, sharing our needs, sharing prayer requests, updating each other on our travels and ministries."[3] This relationship was regular, intentional, and occasionally uncomfortable. "As a friend, I had asked Ravi pointed questions on at least two occasions. He had given me his rehearsed answers, both over the phone and face to face," this same friend wrote.[4]

Ravi's dishonesty intensified his isolation. Ravi wasn't honest with this friend, with colleagues who encouraged him to stop traveling with a masseuse, or, seemingly, with anyone. It seems that he had no real relationships in which he believed he could be fully known.

The twelve-page investigative report detailing just a sampling of Ravi's transgressions included one victim's disturbing statement that Ravi told her not to come forward with any allegations against him or she would be responsible for the potential "millions of souls" whose salvation would be at risk if his reputation were damaged.[5] It was a terrible, manipulative weight to put on a victim's shoulders. But perhaps that's the weight that Ravi himself carried. Perhaps he saw no path to confession and truth-telling without great risk to his— and God's—reputation.

Beyond the typical feelings of pride and shame that hold all of us back from confession, leaders have an additional layer to think about: How will this affect those I lead? To be clear, there is no excuse or justification for this type of hidden life, and this argument cannot excuse Ravi's consistent, ongoing patterns of abuse. But I can see in Ravi the same current I've seen in lesser-known leaders that actively pulls them away from truth-telling, leaving them isolated and alone. "There's a gravitational pull toward isolation in leadership," writes author Carey Nieuwhof.[6] The Johari Window is a psychological tool developed by Joseph Luft and Harrington Ingham to help individuals diminish the gap between their self-perception and others' perception of them. It consists of four quadrants: an open area, known to ourselves and others; an unknown area, not known to self or others; a blind spot, known to others but not ourselves; and a hidden area, known to ourselves but not to others. We all have aspects of our character or behavior that fall into each of these categories. Ravi's open area would have included his eloquence, intellectual capacity, ministry work, and dedication to apologetics. His unknown area may have included undiscovered talents or weaknesses, repressed memories, and areas of unconsciousness. His blind area may have included his growing arrogance and effect on others. And his hidden area—including private thoughts, feelings, and undisclosed experiences—housed the secrets that eventually undermined his credibility and legacy.

Ravi kept huge parts of his life, calendar, and relationships concealed from even those closest to him. His ability to rationalize an expansive hidden area allowed him to maintain a façade of moral integrity while engaging in misconduct that belied his public stance. Ravi was admired by millions, and a pedestal is perhaps the most dangerous place for a human being to be: elevated, isolated, and extremely vulnerable to the attacks of an enemy who "prowls around like a roaring lion looking for someone to devour" (1 Peter 5:8).

I think of the haunting words of a safari guide on a recent visit to Akagera National Park in Rwanda. He pointed to a lone gazelle grazing on the savanna and asked our group, "Do you know what that is called?"

"Gazelle!" someone helpfully offered.

"Dinner," he replied.

NO REAL FRIENDS

When we read about King David in Scripture, we read about friends, confidants, and counselors. When David was discouraged by his opponents, Jonathan strengthened his faith in God. When David committed adultery and murder, Nathan made him face his guilt. When David proudly suggested taking a census of his fighting men, Joab rebuked his plan. We also see multiple mentions of a man named Hushai, who was David's confidant.

Solomon, too, had a confidant: Zabud. Zabud, however, gets just one mention—a passing record of his existence—in Solomon's story (1 Kings 4:5). What happened to Zabud? Did Solomon, in all his wisdom, find himself needless of counselors and confidants? Was Zabud sidelined for speaking truths Solomon didn't want to hear? We can only speculate.

Likewise, there's no scriptural record of prophets advising Solomon, though both Nathan and Ahijah lived during his reign. There are no indicators that in the prime of his life Solomon had prophets or friends willing to inflict "faithful wounds" to his vanity or self-indulgence. He seems to have ruled alone.

What a contrast to his father.

Even though David massively lost his way, he was rebuked and returned. Solomon, uncorrected, went off course and stayed there.

Throughout Ecclesiastes, Solomon writes multiple times, "What is the gain?" He uses the Hebrew word *yitron*, a business term that speaks of profit, earnings, and capital gains. It's found nowhere else in the Bible, and its repeated use in Ecclesiastes seems to reveal

Solomon's overly commercial worldview. To him, everything is supposed to yield *yitron*.

Many of us share that particular vision. It comes out in our language, as we bring business concepts into nonbusiness contexts through expressions like, "Let's get down to business" and "Mind your own business." We're making *value propositions* all the time. We want to *net* results in everything we do. *Bottom line*: we're always casting things in commercial terms (all puns intended).

But in Ecclesiastes 4, Solomon writes from a different perspective:

> Two are better than one, because they have a good return for their labor: If either of them falls down, one can help the other up. But pity anyone who falls and has no one to help them up. . . . Though one may be overpowered, two can defend themselves. A cord of three strands is not quickly broken. (vv. 9-10, 12)

He describes friendship in noncommercial terms. Even the phrase "good return" or "good reward" isn't *yitron*. There's gain in friendship beyond what can be described in cash value terms—help, warmth, security.

These words, written near the end of his life, represent a dawning realization, a departure from how he seems to have lived his life.

TRUSTED FRIENDS

Survey the leadership landscape and it can look like too many islands, too few island chains.

What if Solomon's and our default was set to truth-telling with trusted friends? What if Ravi had a group of friends with whom he was honest about his struggles? What if he saw growth in his hidden area as an early warning sign, causing him to pause, ask difficult questions, and invite trusted friends to discern with him recalibrations that were needed to come back into missional alignment? What if he followed the counsel of James 5:16 to "confess your sins to each other and pray for each other so that you may be healed"? Might he have received targeted accountability, structural safeguards, and prayer support that could have caused him to change course and prevent harmful actions?

He lost out on real friendships, and he lost his way.

The statement released by Ravi's board in response to the devastating findings read, "We allowed our misplaced trust in Ravi to result in him having less oversight and accountability than would have been wise and loving."[7] While offering one another accountability can feel uncomfortable and unpleasant, "loving" is the right word to describe it. As Proverbs 27:6 says, "Wounds from a friend can be trusted."

Have we given trusted friends permission to inflict wounds that might just save us from tremendous self-harm?

Mark DeMoss, a public relations professional who served faith-based organizations and causes for nearly three decades, wrote in *Christianity Today*,

> After managing hundreds of crises of every conceivable kind, I found that almost every one could have been prevented. Except for acts of nature, terrorism, or crime, the worst crises inevitably stem from self-inflicted wounds, mistakes that might have been avoided had there been an accountability structure with voices to say no.[8]

Truth-telling—and truth receiving—is inherently risky. Most of us are neither eager to offend our friends nor to let go of our own carefully crafted personas and put our real selves out there to be criticized or rejected. But what's difficult is also what's needed. Knowing how important real friendships are, I have invited a small group of lifelong friends to call me out—and they are not afraid to do so. Sometimes they seem to enjoy it, and sometimes I do not, but I know it's a gift.

The Evangelical Council for Financial Accountability, historically a group focused on *financial* accountability, recently released new leadership standards that will become a part of their future accreditation process. They explain their rationale:

> Far too many leaders are struggling in isolation as they face the unique pressures, demands, and challenges of ministry leadership. There has been a notable rise in reports of burnout, leaders leaving the ministry, and other tragic integrity failures. All these have devastating consequences for leaders, their families, their communities, and the gospel witness of the church. . . . Integrity failures pose one of the greatest financial risks to churches and ministries today.[9]

Would stories of drift be less common if stories of friendship and truth-telling were more common?

YOUR SOUL > YOUR MINISTRY

Priscilla Shirer recalls a conversation with Nancy DeMoss Wolgemuth, in which Nancy expressed her deep gratitude for board members and mentors who cared more about her soul than her ministry.

Priscilla says this type of relationship is vital. "We all need to be covered by someone who cares more about the state of our soul than they do our ministry." Priscilla refers to this as a "covenant relationship," in which trusted friends are free to ask us about "the hidden places," require answers, and offer godly counsel that prioritizes our soul, not our ministry. "I think that's been one of the biggest hiccups for church leaders today is that we're not all surrendered to some authority in our life who is discipling us and making sure that we're okay not just in the public parts, but in the private parts of our life."[10]

In his classic work *Celebration of Discipline*, Richard Foster characterizes confession among "the corporate disciplines."[11] It's a noteworthy classification since we confess our sins directly to God. But Foster compellingly argues the value of confessing to God in the presence of a trusted friend.

Isolation and sin work hand in hand. Unconfessed sin prevents us from wholly entering into community, ensuring there is always a part of ourselves that we are holding back, even when we appear engaged. Unconfessed sin isolates. It is equally true that sin thrives in isolation. As Dietrich Bonhoeffer wrote,

> Sin demands to have a man by himself. It withdraws him from the community. The more isolated a person is, the more destructive will be the power of sin over him, and the more deeply he becomes involved in it, the more disastrous is his isolation. Sin wants to remain unknown. It shuns the light.[12]

But confession doesn't allow it. It grabs hold of sin, dragging it into the light where it can be seen, known, and robbed of its power. "As long as I am by myself in the confession of my sins everything remains in the dark," Bonhoeffer wrote, "but in the presence of a brother the sin has to be brought into the light."[13]

There is no better way to reduce the risk of self-inflicted harm resulting from the blind and hidden areas of the Johari Window than radical candor with trusted friends. Andy Crouch has said, "We're meant to have people in our lives who are so close to us that nothing can impress them and nothing can shock them."[14] We need a small group of people who love us enough to ask the uncomfortable questions, listen with a nonjudgmental spirit, and call out our half truths or spin. And we have to commit to reducing the hidden areas of our lives and letting in the light, recognizing the wisdom and the gift of confession. How many leaders would not lose their way if they were walking alongside trusted companions committed to a lifetime of friendship and regular connection?

Not long ago, I shared a challenge and the way I thought I might address it with a friend. He listened intently and then, with a smile, responded, "Hey Pete, you're being an idiot." That's a good friend. Followers and fans are insufficient. To live on mission, we need trusted friends.

PRAYER

Holy and awesome God,
    I don't want to fail you,
    I don't want to shame your name,
      my family, my team, your church, your kingdom.
But I am weak at times and arrogant at others.
In moments of temptation and compromise
    I need help,
    I need honesty,
    I need community,
    I need friendship,
    I need mentoring,
    I need you.
Protect me from my sinful desires.
Protect my heart from deceit and lies.
Humble me, Lord.

So I can hear from you.

So I can hear the warnings of those around me.

So I can respond, repent, and grow.

Lead me not into temptation;

    deliver me from evil,

      so I may one day join the great cloud of witnesses

      and hear you say the most important words I could ever hear:

    "Well done, good and faithful servant."

—Ryan Skoog

FINDING OUR WAY— RELATIONAL CONSTELLATION MAP

Consider the layers of your present relationships and use the visual to chart your relationships.[15]

- *Core four*: Who are your four closest friends? Who do you trust to be a truth-teller to you? List their names, or ask God who he might be inviting you to bring into your inner circle.

- *Mentors*: Who are you learning from across the disciplines of your life and work? Rather than identifying one supercharged mentor, choose to learn from a variety of people. Identify mentors for the areas that matter most to you: spiritual, relational, financial, etc. List the names of the individuals you are learning from or would like to learn from.

- *Mentees*: Who are you pouring into? Who are the aspiring leaders with whom you can share your own experiences to invest in their growth?

- *Prayer partners*: Who is praying for you? These individuals are invested in your spiritual, emotional, social, and personal health. Write the names of prayer advocates in your life or ask

God to bring names to mind of those who would be willing to regularly intercede for you in prayer.

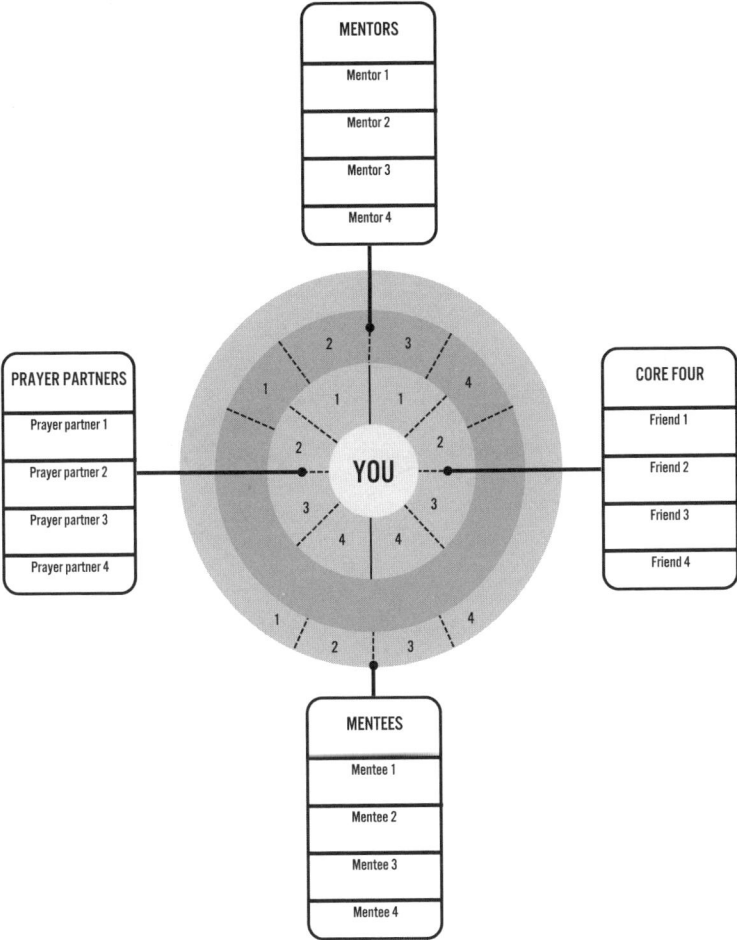

MENTORS

| Mentor 1 |
| Mentor 2 |
| Mentor 3 |
| Mentor 4 |

PRAYER PARTNERS

| Prayer partner 1 |
| Prayer partner 2 |
| Prayer partner 3 |
| Prayer partner 4 |

YOU

CORE FOUR

| Friend 1 |
| Friend 2 |
| Friend 3 |
| Friend 4 |

MENTEES

| Mentee 1 |
| Mentee 2 |
| Mentee 3 |
| Mentee 4 |

10

SELF AT THE CENTER

Preach the gospel, die, and be forgotten.

Nikolaus Ludwig von Zinzendorf

My daughter was giddy, shouting across the golden sand as she raced down the beach. "Daddy, come quick!" Lili and I had just arrived in Newport Beach, California, and she was more than a little enthusiastic to touch the ocean. The sun was setting in a breathtaking haze of purples and golds. Not wanting to waste a second of remaining light, we hastily tossed our shoes, rolled up our jeans, and sprinted into the waves.

At six o'clock the next morning, Lili was in her bathing suit and ready to go again. We were the first two people to feel the morning dew on our feet and see the foam collecting in whirl-pools on the shore. Learning to surf proved far more difficult than anticipated, so in lieu of riding waves, we decided to build a sandcastle.

With a few basic tools, we built a magnificent castle. Its central fortress, almost as tall as eight-year-old Lili, was guarded by thick, well-constructed walls. Every other sandcastle we'd ever constructed looked paltry by comparison.

As the morning wore on, I noticed the tide coming in. Lili and I had taken pains to build our castle far from the destructive waves, but we had underestimated the water's reach. Hours of work were under imminent threat.

As one wave washed dangerously close, Lili pleaded, "Daddy, we need to build thicker walls!"

We worked furiously as the unrelenting waves lapped closer and closer. Finally our castle's defenses were breached. A single wave swept away the outer wall, causing one sandy side to collapse.

With greater urgency, Lili shouted, "Quick, Daddy! We need to dig a moat!"

It took exactly one more wave to fill our moat to overflowing. We were no match for the mighty Pacific, and our masterpiece was reduced to soggy mounds. "Daddy, it's all gone," Lili sighed. I never expected it to last forever, but I couldn't help feeling let down by the futility of our efforts.

What happens to castles of sand also happens to castles of stone. Fast or slow, the tide is coming in.

THE IMPERMANENCE OF INFLUENCE

During his lifetime, Solomon had far more influence than most of us ever will. For forty years, he reigned over Israel when it was roughly three times its current size: including parts of present-day Lebanon, Jordan, and Syria. His reputation and fame extended so far beyond the country that the Queen of Sheba traveled from southern Arabia (modern-day Yemen) to see if all she had heard about him was true.

"Not even half was told me; in wisdom and wealth you have far exceeded the report I heard," she summarized (1 Kings 10:7). Everything about Solomon's kingdom seemed designed to impress. But in one regard, Solomon may not have lived up to his reputation. First Kings 10:1 says the Queen of Sheba heard of Solomon's fame *"and his relationship to the LORD"* (emphasis added). His reputation was connected to his relationship with God, but his lifestyle was increasingly not. Her response to his wisdom and wealth was, Praise God! (1 Kings 10:9). But was Solomon seeking God's glory or his own?

Solomon built buildings far grander than any I've inhabited or constructed of sand. If anyone was well positioned to leave a legacy, it was Solomon—and in his early years, he seemed to anticipate one. Solomon referred to the temple he built as "a place for [God] to dwell forever" (2 Chronicles 6:2). The construction project spanned seven years of Solomon's reign and was one of his most famed accomplishments. But he also built a palace that took nearly twice as long (1 Kings 7:1). The author of 1 Kings provides dimensions of both the temple and the palace, and it's hard not to draw a comparison: The palace was more than twice as wide and nearly twice as long as the temple. The house Solomon built for himself dwarfed the house he built for God.

It begs the question, in pursuing a legacy, *Whose house are we building?*

It's in our nature to want to leave a mark on this world. It's the reason everything from bricks to benches to buildings bear the name of those who funded them. Most of the buildings on our nation's university campuses are named for benefactors. I can still rattle off the names adorning the buildings where I lived: Miller, Witmer, Naugle, and Kelly. But I don't know a thing about the people whose names they bear. These folks' good names and life's work were reduced to the places I bunked.

If they built buildings so that they would be remembered, then frankly, it's been a waste. But if they built buildings so that students could live on a campus where their hearts would be stirred, their minds stretched, and their callings clarified, then their legacy is rich indeed. The students who lived in these buildings went on to build families and contribute to society in better ways than they would have otherwise. Some became superintendents of schools and others served among people experiencing poverty. Some built world-class companies and others built widgets, but countless lives were enhanced because they lived in this community in this pivotal season of life. Perhaps we don't need to know Miller or Naugle, and they don't need to be known. Their legacy, like ours, is in God's hands.

The leaders I respect most aren't preoccupied with making a name for themselves. Status and fame are not currencies they value. Celebrity is not a stock they invest in. They aren't building to create a legacy; they build to love and serve God and others. They're focused on a mission that is so much bigger than themselves. They've caught a bigger kingdom vision and are not preoccupied with their own castles made of sand.

RISING FROM ASHES

Mark was a visionary pastor, charismatic communicator, and bold leader. In an underchurched part of the country, he grew a Bible study in his home to a church of nearly fifteen thousand weekly attendees across fifteen campuses over fifteen years. His church became one of the largest and most influential in the country. Then he launched a network to help others plant churches based on his successful model.

Mark was a compelling yet divisive figure, and the rapid rise and precipitous fall of the church he founded has been well documented.[1] The underlying issues and challenges facing the church have been widely debated and discussed, with much said about celebrity culture, lackluster accountability structures, spiritual abuse, and drift. When Mark resigned under pressure, the church experienced a mass exodus of staff, members, and campuses, eventually dissolving as an entity in 2015. His castle crumbled.

But of course that's not the end of the story.

After the church disbanded, some of its former campuses became independent churches that continued to operate under different names and leadership. For the last decade, some have continued to love, serve, and teach. Rising out of the ashes, they seem to have found health and renewed mission. Mark's kingdom collapsed, but God's kingdom endures.

Many of the surviving churches selected names that speak to a process of refining: Foundry, Resurrection, Redemption, Restoration, Grace. Many have simplified their statement of belief and their ministry model, seeking to return to the core elements of faith and life together. These churches haven't made headlines, but those gathered there continue to make an impact, loving God and people despite the pain and trauma many experienced during and after Mark's reign.

Members have discovered, in their words, that the church "wasn't all about one man. It was about Jesus and his mission."[2]

What made the difference between a church that fell into disarray and those that have risen? Might there be a lesson for us in it all?

Perhaps there is nothing new under the sun, and nothing new at this point in the book. In summary, these leaders called their congregations to refocus on their mission. To see beyond themselves. To get back to the beautiful basics. They traded what felt like a leading role in a smaller mission for a smaller role in a far grander story.

These churches are examples of how God can continue to bring life from brokenness as we offer ourselves in service of a mission that extends far beyond ourselves. They remind us that the gospel is not limited to any one institution or leader but goes forth in the extensive power and grace of Jesus Christ. They also remind us that the church is a group of people—not just one leader—on mission together to love God and love our neighbors.

These enduring congregations built vibrant teams and thought beyond themselves. Whether incidentally or intentionally, it seems that those who lasted had a healthy distrust of personal charisma and the concentration of influence in a single individual. Humility, staff development, and a focus on the ultimate mission helped these churches and their lead pastors find their way forward.

One pastor who departed the then-thriving megachurch to focus on church planting shared that while the megachurch was in its prime there had been a presumption that it was the place to be "if you want to be part of what Jesus is doing in our city." But he found the view from outside—and now the view from the rubble—to be different from the view inside. "I was blown away by the million things Jesus was doing in the city which were unnamed and unbranded but just as spectacular."[3]

God is writing spectacular stories—and we play supporting, not starring roles.

THINKING BEYOND OURSELVES

Tim Keller—a bestselling author and celebrity in his own right—seemed wary of celebrity culture and churches' overreliance on a single person. Redeemer, the church Keller founded in New York

City, never announced who was going to be preaching in a particular location. They wanted to ensure that Jesus was the main attraction and the focus of every service.

Keller famously empowered and equipped others to lead, modeling what he preached in *The Freedom of Self-Forgetfulness*: "The essence of gospel-humility is not thinking more of myself or thinking less of myself, it is thinking of myself less."[4]

Ironically, this will take thought and effort. We drift toward self-absorption and myopia, preventing us from seeing the liabilities of what Keller called "addictive dependence" on a founder or charismatic leader.[5] We must consciously, effortfully row in the opposite direction.

I see succession planning as one of the most powerful, practical ways we do that. It's an underappreciated organizational discipline. It seems that too few leaders spend much time thinking beyond themselves and actively investing in future leaders. "According to BoardSource's latest Leading With Intent report . . . only 29 percent of nonprofits surveyed reported that they had a written succession plan in place."[6] There's an alarming absence of formal planning and preparation for the time when we will leave our organizations.

Keller wrote that the same is true within the church. Too many leaders tend to "see the church as their personal possession—and an extension of their personality and self-image. They often never want to leave, nor do they know how to well."[7]

We too seldom think beyond ourselves to develop other leaders in our sphere. Some see potential protégés as outright competition. Others fail to see them at all. Perhaps that is part of the reason why strikingly, only 30 percent of key leadership roles in the nonprofit sector were filled by internal promotion in a recent Bridgespan survey—"about half the rate of for-profits."[8]

But as life coach Susan Brown says, "Life is so much simpler when ego is not involved."[9]

Creating a succession plan seems like a modest starting point to see beyond our ego and to help an organization think beyond our tenure. Succession planning invites and unites our team to refocus on the guiding mission of the organization, which inevitably extends beyond our leadership.

CRUMBLING CASTLES

None of us will lead forever. Solomon died around 931 BC, and what he had labored to build quickly began to crumble.

After Solomon's death, the people of Israel came to his son and heir, Rehoboam, to air their grievances. They said Solomon had ruled harshly, and they pleaded with Rehoboam to lighten their load. Instead, Rehoboam promised a rule still further off mission and still more oppressive than his father's. In response, the kingdom divided, and the Davidic line retained leadership of only the tribes of Judah and Benjamin.

Before a decade had passed, the king of Egypt attacked and "carried off the treasures of the temple of the LORD and the treasures of the royal palace." First Kings 14:26 summarizes, "He took everything." The wealth Solomon stored up was amassed for another (Ecclesiastes 6:2).

It gets worse. Within a few centuries, Nebuchadnezzar, king of Babylon, laid siege to Jerusalem. As 2 Kings 25:9 details, the armies of Babylon raided and razed the palace and the temple Solomon thought would last forever. His anticipated legacy goes up in smoke: "[Nebuzaradan, commander of the imperial guard] set fire to the temple of the LORD, the royal palace and all the houses of Jerusalem." In the grand scheme, Solomon's palace did not last much longer than Lili's castle.

Hevel.

This is precisely the type of outcome that led to Solomon's frustration in Ecclesiastes. Even though he didn't know the specifics of how it would happen, he seemed to know that it would happen. That all he built would one day be dismantled. Through his considerable strengths he tried to make enduring marks on the world. But it was futile: The wealth was stolen, the wisdom abandoned, the buildings demolished.

Too many of us are leading in the way of Solomon, who seems to have never seriously considered what would happen to Israel after he left. He never set a successor up for success.

To the end of his life, it was all about what he could still build. What he could still do. We see no evidence that Solomon stopped to reflect, "You know what, I've probably accomplished enough. It's time for me to pour into the next generation of leaders. To think about what's next for Israel and how to finish well."

He never moved from doing to equipping. From king to coach.

Tragically, Solomon missed the opportunity for real mentorship and leadership development with his son Rehoboam. He did not teach him the wisdom and the ways of the Lord. He did not prepare him for the challenges and responsibilities of ruling a nation. We see no evidence that Solomon facilitated relationships with a council of wise advisers who could guide Rehoboam in the years to come. And most unfortunately, he did not instill in his son a sense of deep faith or humble service. Solomon left a divided and rebellious kingdom with an ill-equipped heir.

Like too many leaders, Solomon started well but finished poorly. The ultimate ending was the glaring absence of a called and equipped next leader. Solomon built great buildings, but we see no evidence that he built great leaders.

Solomon spent his life focused on "me," not "we." It was, and is, the surest way to lose sight of what ultimately matters.

Mission-true leaders are able to think beyond themselves. They see beyond their personal ambition and achievements to a bigger mission. They're able to set their sights on a longer timeline and a larger goal because they see their story as part of a bigger and better story. They focus less on their personal success and the credit they're due and more on what a group of people across generations are able to accomplish together. Their purpose and mission extends beyond their lifetime and abilities.

INTERIM LEADERS

When my son Myles was eight, he came home from school inquiring about the political process in the United States. He was particularly interested in term limits and the four-year election cycle.

With eagerness, he wanted to understand my term as president of a nonprofit and when my term would end. I shared that term limits were only for political offices, not for nonprofits. Furrowing his brow he questioned, "So are you like a king or a president?"

For leaders of any sort, it's easy for us to act like little kings trying to build our little kingdoms. To follow in the ways of Solomon and think no further than our own tenure. To see our successors' flailing or failure as a sign of their weakness rather than our poor handoff. To keep building and doing when we should have moved to equipping and empowering.

We are all interim in our roles. The ultimate appraisal of our success or failure must be measured when we transition.

A few years ago, Chris Horst, who wrote the foreword to this book, transitioned from his staff role at HOPE International after sixteen years of collaboration and several shared writing projects. At the end of a staff retreat, he pulled me aside to initiate a conversation that I hoped would never happen. He shared that it was time to move from staff to donor. He was going to leave HOPE so that he could focus on caring for his family while his wife, Alli, took an expanded leadership role in her workplace.

At the time, Chris oversaw our fundraising, strategy, and spiritual integration. Internally and externally, he was loved and respected for his consistent focus on HOPE's gospel integration. I knew we would remain lifelong friends, but given Chris's influence, tenure, and trust, I wondered what would happen at HOPE.

In what I believe was the ultimate sign of success, when Chris left, we missed him for his friendship, not his function. Chris had invested in his team and the leaders coming after him so well that, operationally, his departure was seamless. The right people with the same heart for our mission were in place and undoubtedly prepared for their new roles. The highest compliment I can give to Chris is that because of his incredible leadership and the way he equipped his teammates-turned-successors, HOPE has continued to grow in his absence. This is what it looks like to finish well in our organizational missions in service of a grander mission.

Chris's model inspired me to consider what more I could do to prepare for the moment when it will be my turn to transition. Because I care deeply about HOPE's team and mission, I want to do everything possible to set my successors up for success. While I do not know when that day will come, I do know that today I'm one day closer to that transition than I was yesterday.

As a first step, we started making succession planning a regular topic of conversation at HOPE. Every January I submit a list of five names to the board of directors. Each name represents a person I believe would do an exceptional job in my role and includes specific assignments and growth opportunities for each potential successor. While the list is confidential, the process is not, and we've replicated the practice throughout the organization with every leader across HOPE.

The irony is that this process is not just an organizational practice; it is deeply personal. Considering my potential successors shapes my own heart, plans, and priorities, reminding me that one day this will not be an exercise but a reality. It allows me to hold less tightly to this current role, remembering that there are others who will sit at "my" desk and make decisions differently. It allows me to pause and pray for others and for the long-term missional alignment of this organization. Succession planning shapes my heart.

We are all interim leaders. When we are animated by the bigger mission, we can shift to a posture of supporting and equipping others, knowing that someday we will transition, another will step into our role, and we will get to cheer them on.

THE LITTLE, LEAST, AND LAST LAST

Part of the adventure of living for God and not ourselves is that we never know what will leave a lasting mark. But God being who he is, it probably will be something unexpected.

Whose gift is the standard of generosity: King David, who dedicated his kingly fortune to the temple or the poor, nameless woman who put two pennies in the collection (1 Chronicles 29; Luke 21:1-4)?

Whose worship was more immortalized: the high priest who entered the Most Holy Place on the Day of Atonement to offer sacrifices on behalf of the nation or the woman who anointed Jesus' feet from her alabaster jar of perfume (Leviticus 16; Luke 7:36-38)?

Whose faith stands as the greater model: Elijah, who called down fire from heaven or the centurion who said to Jesus, "Lord, . . . just say the word, and my servant will be healed" (2 Kings 1:10; Matthew 8:5-10)?

So often it's the little things done by the littler people that leave the lasting mark.

Pursuing our own legacy is, as Solomon discovered, chasing after the wind. But that doesn't mean that life is without meaning and purpose. Far from it. It means we should live for God and become a small part in a much grander mission. Most of what we build will be left to someone else. It may be torn down, mismanaged, undervalued, or misunderstood. We can't know what will happen. As Solomon put it, "Who can tell [a person] what will happen under the sun after they are gone?" (Ecclesiastes 6:12).

Solomon couldn't have known and wouldn't have anticipated what his legacy would be. It wasn't his alliances, wealth, or military might that God chose to work through. When we think of Solomon today, what has endured is his God-given wisdom and his words. When we take his teachings to heart, God continues to work redemptively through his legacy, making meaning where Solomon couldn't.

Human beings are role players in an epic drama. God directs, Jesus stars, and we stand as townspeople in a cast of thousands. If we yearn for more of the stage, we'll likely be frustrated. We'll feel insignificant and trudge through our scenes with uninspired performance. But God has made—and will make—"everything beautiful in its time" (Ecclesiastes 3:11), including our fleeting moments and brief lines. A subplot in Jesus' climactic scene guarantees it.

One of the criminals crucified with Christ was a revolutionary against Rome. Talk about futile work! In many ways he typifies a wasted life, and we do not even know his name. But during his brief moment on stage, he uttered a line that goes down as one of the greatest in history: "Jesus, remember me when you come into your kingdom" (Luke 23:42).

Boom. One moment of clarity in a life of futility and everything changes.

We sometimes note how a legacy and reputation, carefully built over many years or decades, can be destroyed in a moment. That's true, of course, and we do well to remember it, but do we ever consider how a legacy and reputation can be *established* in a moment?

That's a rarer occurrence, to be sure, but it can happen. The anonymous "thief on the cross" proves it. His *magnum opus*, his great work, was asking to be remembered—not for his cause or achievements but for his faith—right in the moment when Rome was obliterating him. And so he became Exhibit A that it's never too late to turn around.

Has anyone ever used his dying breath more wisely?

PRAYER

Eternal Jesus,
    may the end goal of my life be what lasts forever
Your glory alone.
Your story alone.
Your power alone.
Your presence alone.
Your words alone.
Your kingdom alone.
For your name alone.
May I give the very best of my few days to you.
May the short breath of my life be a resounding "Hallelujah"
    for the ages.

All things are from you, all things are to you, all things are for you,
  Jesus, Lord forever.
Amen.

—Ryan Skoog

FINDING OUR WAY—
SUCCESSION PLANNING CHECKLIST

- ***Start the conversation***: If you haven't already, begin the conversation about succession planning with a small group of trusted advisers. We are all only interim in our roles, so let's normalize the conversation and the reality that one day, we will all transition. State your desire for the organization to thrive after your inevitable departure.

- ***Don't put off the hard stuff***: If your successor entered your role tomorrow, what would need to be cleaned up for them today? Consider any staffing or organizational processes that may merit review. What would need to happen to make sure they are set up for success?

- ***Identify potential successors***: Identify people who could do your job well and who you believe fit the profile of a successful leader. Review the names annually.

- ***Empower others***: Find ways to regularly share opportunities with potential successors to help them grow and develop into your leadership role. Consider creating an annual plan of tasks or opportunities you could give away to growing leaders.

- ***Retreat***: Consider going away for a twenty-four-hour retreat at least once a year. As part of the retreat, spend time surrendering your position to God and asking for clarity if it might be time to consider a transition.

- *Notice your fears*: Make a list of the fears you have when you think about your transition. After writing your list, find biblical truths to combat each fear as it relates to your identity and calling. Share the list with close friends or family and allow them to speak into each item you named.

- *Create or review an emergency succession plan*: In the event of a sudden departure, modify the stages above. Consider identifying and appointing an interim leader in the case of an emergency.

CONCLUSION

FEW FINISH WELL

Few, they tell me, finish well . . .
Lord, let me get home before dark.

ROBERTSON MCQUILKEN

God has never appeared to me in a dream, inviting me to ask for my heart's desire, as he invited Solomon, but it's an interesting exercise to think about what my request might be. *What is the deepest desire of my heart?* Would I approach the opportunity reverently or treat God like a sanctified genie?

Solomon could have asked for his enemies to be humiliated, his kingdom to prosper, or his own name to be revered. In contrast, his request for wisdom was both just and humble. First Kings 3:10 says the Lord "was pleased" with his request—and God granted it.

But fast-forward to the end of his life, and wisdom is just another thing Solomon calls *hevel.* His chief pursuit turned out to be as meaningless as all the rest.

Solomon and the modern leaders who have followed in his foot-steps pursued—and often received from God—many of the things that I, too, have wanted and even prayed for, but their stories didn't end well. They lost their way amid strong currents or in pursuit of their hearts' desires. Perhaps that's why Solomon counseled in Proverbs 4:23, "Above all else, guard your heart, for everything you do flows from it."

Good leaders veered off course—often in pursuit of good things. *Why should I think it would be any different for me?*

As I've studied Solomon's life, I've become convinced that al-though Solomon asked for something noble, he could have asked for something far better.

At the end of his life, Solomon wrote, "Here is the conclusion of the matter: Fear God and keep his commandments" (Ecclesi-astes 12:13). What if Solomon had made *that* his request? *God, make me a leader who fears you and keeps your commandments.*

What if that was *our* request?

REVERENCE

Solomon wrote in Proverbs 9:10, "The fear of the Lord is the be-ginning of wisdom."

To fear the Lord is to revere him. It's to recognize the truth of his nature, driving us toward God and our need for him. It prompts us to seek help—not just in a one-time request for wisdom but every day, throughout the day. James 1:5 assures us that the wisdom of God is still accessible to us, just as it was to Solomon: "If any of you lacks wisdom, you should ask God, who gives generously to all without finding fault, and it will be given to you." The fear of the Lord in-vites us to respond to our insufficiency by seeking his all-sufficiency. To ensure our mission is not just God-given but God-driven. To keep our eyes on the One who entrusted us with a role to play in a greater story.

It's our fear of the Lord that allows us to recognize the truth of Isaiah 55:8-9: "'For my thoughts are not your thoughts, neither are your ways my ways,' declares the LORD. 'As the heavens are higher than the earth, so are my ways higher than your ways and my thoughts than your thoughts.'" Wise king that he was, Solomon did not bow or bend his will to one still wiser. He did not keep God's commands when they contradicted common wisdom. How often could the same be said of us?

As leaders, we lose our way when our fear of the Lord is insufficient to prompt us to keep his commands. Researching this book, Jill and I expected to find leaders pulled off mission by a single misguided pursuit or strong current, one specific struggle or besetting sin. But in one example after another, we discovered that once we have lost our fear of the Lord, we, like Solomon, don't stop with a single misguided pursuit. Once we have contravened God's commands in one area, we are well on our way to the next, unless we intentionally course correct. Rather than living and leading on mission, we begin to meander. The distance between our path and our intended destination grows as we fail to fear God and keep his commands in one small choice after another. This pattern becomes ingrained as muscle memory until adherence to God's commands no longer significantly shapes our decision-making.

But we can also build the muscle memory of obedience. Just as each unfaithful decision subtly turns our rudder off mission, each faithful decision guides us back on course, where God's grace and forgiveness are waiting. Few leaders finish well, but we don't have to resign ourselves to ending poorly. We are invited to keep looking toward our desired destination and then row, row, row. Those who finish well *aim* to finish well, and they look to a king far wiser than Solomon to show them the way.

A DIFFERENT KING

Roughly two centuries after Solomon died, the prophet Isaiah promised that another king was coming to reign. This king would be unlike any other. "The Spirit of the LORD will rest on him—the Spirit of wisdom and of understanding, the Spirit of counsel and of might, the Spirit of the knowledge and fear of the LORD," Isaiah says. "And he will delight in the fear of the LORD" (Isaiah 11:2-3).

Jesus came to do what Solomon did not: to "delight in the fear of the LORD." We seldom link fear and delight. On the surface they seem antithetical, but Isaiah connects Jesus' *knowledge* of the Lord to his *fear* of the Lord. Jesus knew God intimately, walked in obedience, and delighted in the relationship with his Father.

Jesus began his ministry with forty days of fasting and prayer in the wilderness (Matthew 4). Putting ourselves in Jesus' shoes, we often imagine how weak he must have been from the physical deprivation, but we seldom think of how spiritually strong Jesus would have been as he prepared to emerge from that wilderness retreat. Abstaining from food, Jesus feasted on time with his Father. At the end of this time, Satan appeared to Jesus with three temptations.

There are many ways to interpret the temptations of Jesus. Hebrews 4:15 says that Jesus was tempted in every way that we are, so perhaps we are each meant to find relevance to our personal struggles in the example of Jesus' temptations. Henri Nouwen summarized them as the temptations to be relevant, spectacular, and powerful.[1] Gerald Griffin, an elder and teaching pastor at Bridgetown Church, believes Jesus' temptations were fundamentally attacks on his mission and purpose, and that like us, he needed to hear the Father define his true identity.[2] When we consider them, Jesus' temptations are struggles each leader will face.

In the temptations of Jesus, we see the overarching motivations behind Solomon's misguided pursuits—and ours.

1. "If you are the Son of God, tell these stones to become bread" (Matthew 4:3). Satisfy your appetites: What you crave is yours for the taking. You deserve it. Don't deny yourself anything you desire.

2. "If you are the Son of God . . . throw yourself down. For it is written: 'He will command his angels concerning you . . . so that you will not strike your foot against a stone'" (Matthew 4:6). Prove yourself: Your value is assigned by others; make sure people highly regard you.

3. The devil showed Jesus all the kingdoms of the world. "'All this I will give you,' he said, 'if you will bow down and worship me'" (Matthew 4:9). Bypass God's plan: Pursue success on your own terms. There is no wrong path to the right destination.

In these temptations we hear echoes of Satan's original question, undermining Eve's trust in her Creator: *Did God really say . . . ?* Did he really say that we cannot pursue any means to a desired end? Did he really say that we benefit from limits? Did he really say that unmet appetites should drive us to pursue fullness in him?

Jesus modeled a different response to the temptations than Solomon's: fear God and keep his commands. Jesus trusted, quoting Scripture back to Satan, yet again living in alignment with his mission.

That's very good news. Because Jesus chose rightly, when we choose wrongly we are still covered in his grace.

Aware of our propensity to wander, God still invites us to follow. Knowing we succumb to self-gratification and self-aggrandizing, God still calls us. He's filled our Scriptures with stories of imperfect leaders like Solomon, not so we can sit back in smug self-satisfaction but so we can see how his power is made perfect in weaknesses (2 Corinthians 12:9).

I think of the "Hall of Faith" in Hebrews 11: Abel, Enoch, Noah, Abraham, Sarah. These were far from perfect people, but the writer says, "All these people were still living by faith when they died." What an epithet! They saw incredible evidence of God's work, but Hebrews says, "They did not receive the things promised; they only saw them and welcomed them from a distance" (v. 13). That may be true of us as well.

Because this story is God's and not ours, it does not end when we retire from our roles or even when we pass away. God's beautiful story is still being written. May it be said of us that we didn't lose our way, that we lived by faith and finished well.

NOW ALL HAS BEEN HEARD . . . WHAT DO WE DO?

At the end of his life, Solomon was filled with remorse and regret. He looked back on all he had accomplished and realized too late that he had lost his way. He spent his life building a gilded kingdom that would crumble. He wanted to establish a great name for himself, but he's remembered as a king who drifted from his mission and his vibrant relationship with God. Pleasure and profit, power and prestige: in his final chapter, the wisest king called them worthless. *Hevel.*

I fear that too many leaders today have modeled their lives after Solomon's pursuits rather than his conclusion. We rise early, charging into our strategic plans and to-do lists with the ardor of a king going off to war. We try to build our little kingdoms that will make a lasting impact on the world.

But few leaders finish well. We're waylaid by small compromises. Shortcuts. Justifications. Cracks in our character. We realize in retrospect that we chased the wind and missed what mattered.

So the question for you and me today is simply this: What do we need to do? Where do we need to repent and realign our actions and attitudes? How might we have the courage to course correct when we realize we are drifting and the wisdom to establish safeguards that keep us from losing our way? It takes an abundance of God's grace, constant recalibration, and intentionality. As Mark DeMoss wrote, "No one finishes well by accident, of that I'm certain."[3]

On the day Jill and I learned to row, we were delayed in getting on the water because something important had gone missing. "Have you seen the FUS?" our instructor asked one colleague after another. After several minutes of fruitless searching—for exactly what I wasn't sure—I wanted to know, "What's a FUS?"

I smiled at God's sense of humor when the instructor responded, "It's short for the name of the boat: *Finish Up Strong*."

May God grant us wisdom and courage to live on mission—and may we finish up strong.

FINDING OUR WAY—
PROTECTING OUR MISSION

If we desire to be among those few who finish well, we would be wise to safeguard our mission.

Picture your heart as an ancient city that requires protection from attacks. The mission-true practices discussed in this book are designed to help safeguard the city. Use the illustration to assess the strength of your city walls. Fill in the walls with high numbers representing areas of relative strength and low numbers representing areas of vulnerability.

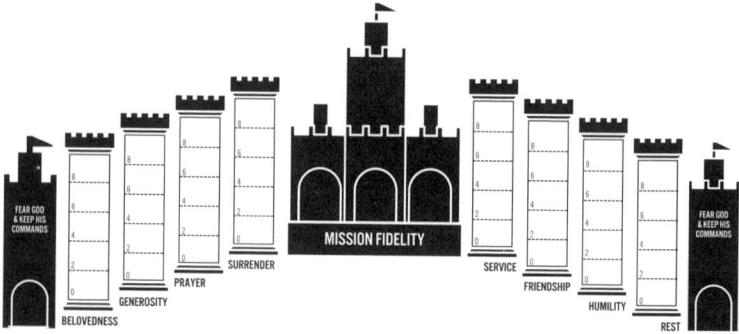

Evaluate: Which "walls" did you rate the highest? Which did you rate the lowest? Consider inviting a close friend or mentor you trust to share their perspective on your vulnerabilities. How might they modify your ratings?

Act: In prayer, ask God for direction and discipline to make changes that will reduce your vulnerability. Consider any actions or next steps the Holy Spirit may be prompting in you. Write them down.

_____

_____

_____

_____

_____

_____

_____

_____

Pray through King Solomon's closing words from Ecclesiastes 12:13-14:

> Now all has been heard;
>> here is the conclusion of the matter:
>
> Fear God and keep his commandments,
>> for this is the duty of all mankind.
>
> For God will bring every deed into judgment,
>> including every hidden thing,
>> whether it is good or evil.

Ask God to fill you with a full and true desire to lead a life of obedience and long-term faithfulness.

For a more robust assessment related to this final exercise, as well as additional resources and tools to help protect your mission, visit www.howleaderslosetheirway.com.

ACKNOWLEDGMENTS

Parts of this book were originally published under the title *40/40 Vision*, coauthored by Greg Lafferty. His words echo throughout this book. Thank you, Greg, for your sermon series so many years ago that started this journey and awakened my fascination with the book of Ecclesiastes.

We are grateful for the willingness of InterVarsity Press to take another angle at King Solomon's story. Al Hsu, our anonymous reviewer, Collin Huber, and the IVP team, thank you for your skill, editing, and insights, which made this a much stronger book. From the original version to this revised project, working with your team has been a gift.

LeAnna Vinc created the tools at the end of each chapter and provided encouragement, creative direction, and research and writing support. Lindsey Reichert served as an intern, researching the life of Solomon and his shifting perspectives from Proverbs to Ecclesiastes. Ryan Skoog contributed compelling ideas and penned the prayers included at the end of each chapter. We're grateful for his friendship and deeply moved by his prayers for us.

In many ways, this book is a continuation of the research and writing for *Mission Drift*. Thank you to Chris Horst and Anna Haggard for the work a decade ago that continues to keep us motivated to live and lead on mission.

Early feedback on the book was provided by my new Australian friends at Christian Venues Association, Peter Dobbs, and our incredible colleagues at HOPE International. Additional feedback and guidance on this book were provided by Pat Ryan, Joe Leininger, Beth Fisher, and Claire Brosius. Thank you to Dan Smucker and Lancaster Log Cabin for the perfect writing location. Once again, Jeff Rutt and the HOPE International board of directors offered encouragement and support for the writing journey—thank you!

Andrew Wolgemuth, thank you for being an outstanding literary agent and a friend. We're so grateful you saw the potential in this book idea.

To our families (for Peter: Laurel, Keith, Liliana, Myles, and London, and for Jill: Bryan, Adelyn, and Celia), you have been so patient as we worked on this project. Special thanks to Jill's cat, Puffin, who provided the background "music" for so many of our calls and conversations.

And finally, thank you, Jesus, for your grace when we, too, have lost our way. *Soli Deo gloria.*

NOTES

INTRODUCTION: WHEN MISSION DRIFT BECOMES PERSONAL

[1] Peter Greer and Chris Horst, *Mission Drift* (Bloomington, MN: Bethany House, 2014), 15.

[2] Robert Robinson, "Come, Thou Fount of Every Blessing," 1758, https://hymnary.org /text/come_thou_fount_of_every_blessing.

1. THE DANGER OF DRIFT

[1] Saint Benedict, *The Rule of St. Benedict in English*, ed. Timothy Fry (Collegeville, MN: Liturgical Press, 2019), 28.

[2] J. Robert Clinton, "Listen Up Leaders!" (Barnabas Publishers, 1989), 7, https:// clintonleadership.com/resources/complimentary/ListenUpLeaders.pdf. Not all the leaders Clinton identified were described in enough detail to be evaluated, but of those who were, only about 30 percent finished well by Clinton's definition. Although Clinton conducted his research decades ago, there's no reason to believe that what has been true for millennia has changed in recent years.

[3] J. Robert Clinton, *The Making of a Leader*, 2nd ed. (Colorado Springs, CO: NavPress, 2012), 242.

[4] Augustine, *The City of God*, trans. Marcus Dods (Peabody, MA: Hendrickson Publishers, 2009), 461.

[5] Tom Brady, "Tom Brady's Patriots Hall of Fame Induction Ceremony Speech," June 13, 2024, https://youtu.be/0bnd_K3dhRk?si=CbRLn6lYCrRRmw_O.

[6] Oliver Wendell Holmes Jr., "On Receiving the Degree of Doctor of Laws" (Yale University Commencement, June 30, 1886), as quoted in Richard. A. Posner, ed., *The Essential Holmes* (Chicago: University of Chicago Press, 1992), 96.

[7] Jim Collins, *How the Mighty Fall* (New York: HarperCollins, 2009), 24-25.

2. MEETING OUR MENTOR

[1] Those who have studied Ecclesiastes will know that its authorship is disputed. Whether or not Solomon authored Ecclesiastes, our teacher in the book is indisputably meant to be identified as King Solomon. Our first hint is his introduction as the "son of David, king in Jerusalem" (Ecclesiastes 1:1). Solomon was David's son and became king directly upon his father's death. Later, we read that this person grew and "increased in wisdom more than anyone who has ruled over Jerusalem before" (Ecclesiastes 1:16). Throughout this book, we're going to simply refer to Solomon as the author of Ecclesiastes.

[2] We see Solomon's awareness of the dangers of pride in verses like Proverbs 16:18: "Pride goes before destruction, a haughty spirit before a fall" and Proverbs 29:23: "Pride brings a person low, but the lowly in spirit gain honor."

[3] "H1892—hebel—Strong's Hebrew Lexicon (KJV)," *Blue Letter Bible*, accessed December 7, 2024, www.blueletterbible.org/lexicon/h1892/kjv/wlc/0-1/.

[4] Jim Collins, *How the Mighty Fall* (New York: HarperCollins, 2009), 119.

[5] Katelyn Beaty, *Celebrities for Jesus* (Grand Rapids, MI: Brazos, 2022), 166.

3. THE ALLURE OF ACHIEVEMENT

[1] Daniel Ladinsky, "St. Thomas Aquinas," in *Love Poems from God: Twelve Sacred Voices from the East and West* (New York: Penguin Group, 2002), 122.

[2] Corinne Benicka, *Great Modern Masters* (New York: Excalibur Books, 1980), 130.

[3] Nicolas Brasch, *Leonardo Da Vinci: The Greatest Inventor* (New York: The Rosen Publishing Group, 2014), 7.

[4] Leonard Woolf, *The Journey Not the Arrival Matters: An Autobiography of the Years 1939 to 1969* (United Kingdom: Harcourt Brace Jovanovich, 1975), 158.

[5] Lulu Garcia-Navarro, "The Interview: Robert Putnam Knows Why You're Lonely," *New York Times*, July 13, 2024, www.nytimes.com/2024/07/13/magazine/robert-putnam-interview.html.

[6] Philip Graham Ryken, *Ecclesiastes: Why Everything Matters* (Wheaton, IL: Crossway, 2010), 48-49.

[7] Henri J. M. Nouwen, "A New Life among the Handicapped," *New Oxford Review*, September 1986, www.newoxfordreview.org/documents/a-new-life-among-the-handicapped/.

[8] Henri J. M. Nouwen, *Life of the Beloved: Spiritual Living in a Secular World* (New York: Crossroad, 1992), 33.

[9] Nouwen, *Life of the Beloved*, 129.

[10] Nouwen, *Life of the Beloved*, 37.

[11] Nouwen, *Life of the Beloved*, 35-36.

¹²LeBron James, interview by JJ Redick, "What Makes a Great Basketball Player?," *Mind the Game*, March 19, 2024, https://youtu.be/q2XVtWfancQ?si=1JXPXCrfe0G7n9UF.

¹³Timothy Keller, *Making Sense of God* (New York: Penguin, 2018), 91.

¹⁴Peter Dobbs, personal interview with Peter Greer, July 30, 2024.

¹⁵Peter Dobbs, email communication with the authors, January 4, 2025.

¹⁶Dobbs, interview with Greer.

4. THE MASTERY OF MONEY

¹ "The Legacy of TBN," TBN, accessed November 26, 2024, www.tbn.org/about /tbn-legacy.

²Ted Olsen, "LA Times Digs Deeper into TBN's Prosperity Gospel Message," *Christianity Today*, September 1, 2004, www.christianitytoday.com/2004/09/la-times -digs-deeper-into-tbns-prosperity-gospel-message/.

³Warren Cole Smith, "Suits Charge TBN with Illegal Financial Practice," *Baptist Press*, April 9, 2012, www.baptistpress.com/resource-library/news/suits-charge-tbn -with-illegal-financial-practice/.

⁴Erik Eckholm, "Family Battle Offers Glimpse Inside Lavish TV Ministry," *New York Times*, May 5, 2012, www.nytimes.com/2012/05/05/us/tbn-fight-offers -glimpse-inside-lavish-tv-ministry.html.

⁵Leonardo Blair, "TBN Execs Threatened Founder's Granddaughter with Gun, Fired Her for Refusing to Skim $100M of Charitable Assets, Lawsuit Claims," *Christian Post*, February 3, 2015, www.christianpost.com/news/tbn-execs-threatened-founders -granddaughter-with-gun-fired-her-for-refusing-to-skim-100m-of-charitable-assets -lawsuit-claims-133522/.

⁶Eckholm, "Family Battle."

⁷Eckholm, "Family Battle."

⁸James Massola, "Hillsong Accused of Misusing Church Funds to Pay for Private Jets, Luxury Retreats," *Sydney Morning Herald*, March 9, 2023, www.smh.com .au/politics/federal/hillsong-accused-of-misusing-church-funds-to-pay-for-private -jets-luxury-retreats-20230309-p5cqri.html.

⁹Benjamin Kirby (PreachersNSneakers), "Ace embroidered sneaker, $650," Instagram, July 29, 2019, www.instagram.com/p/B0hSNI5BzCJ/?hl=en.

¹⁰Massola, "Hillsong Accused of Misusing Church Funds."

¹¹Barry Bowen, "Estimate: Christian Religious Leaders to Embezzle $86 Billion in 2024," *Trinity Foundation*, March 12, 2024, https://trinityfi.org/investigations /estimate-christian-religious-leaders-to-embezzle-86-billion-in-2024/.

¹²Tim Maurer, "The Financial Wisdom Found in Proverbs," *Forbes*, April 16, 2023, www.forbes.com/sites/timmaurer/2023/04/16/the-financial-wisdom-found -in-proverbs/.

[13]Rabbi Jason Sobel, "What does the Mark of the Beast 666 mean?," February 1, 2022, https://youtu.be/2-rytMLqmis?si=LBIuwhoa-li9fuTN.

[14]Andy Crouch, "You Cannot Serve God & Mammon," Faith Driven Investor, March 10, 2022, 01:25, www.youtube.com/watch?v=8w4TQd_c85I.

[15]Andy Crouch, "You Cannot Serve God & Mammon," 04:45.

[16]Les Christie, "America's Homes Are Bigger than Ever," *CNN Money*, June 5, 2014, http://money.cnn.com/2014/06/04/real_estate/american-home-size.

[17]In 2022, the United States had 283 million registered vehicles and 235 million licensed drivers. See Center for Sustainable Systems, University of Michigan, "Personal Transportation Factsheet," 2024, Pub. No. CSS01-07.

[18]Dean Schabner, "Americans Work More than Anyone," *ABC News*, May 1, 2014, http://abcnews.go.com/US/story?id=93364&page=1.

[19]Patrick Clark, "Hoarder Nation: America's Self-Storage Industry is Booming," *Bloomberg Business*, December 1, 2014, www.bloomberg.com/bw/articles/2014-12-01/cyber-monday-gifts-final-resting-place-self-storage.

[20]John F. Helliwell et. al, eds., "World Happiness Report 2024," University of Oxford Wellbeing Research Centre, 2024, https://worldhappiness.report/ed/2024/happiness-of-the-younger-the-older-and-those-in-between/#ranking-of-happiness-2021-2023.

[21]Chris Heath, "The Unbearable Bradness of Being: Further on Down Brad Pitt's Ramble-on Road," *Rolling Stone*, October 1999.

[22]Andy Crouch, "Detoxing From The Power of Money Over Our Life," Faith Driven Investor, March 10, 2022, 00:15 and 02:24, www.youtube.com/watch?v=Jks7cI4k_18.

[23]Massola, "Hillsong Accused of Misusing Church Funds."

[24]"Statistics on U.S. Generosity," Philanthropy Roundtable, accessed November 25, 2024, www.philanthropyroundtable.org/almanac/statistics-on-u-s-generosity/.

[25]Giving USA Annual Report on Philanthropy, as referenced in Jacob Zinkula and Madison Hoff, "Americans' Donations to Charity Are at a 28-Year Low. Blame Inflation, the Rise of Crowdfunding, and the Decline of Religion," *Business Insider*, July 1, 2023, www.businessinsider.com/why-americans-have-slowed-charitable-donations-religion-gofundme-2023-6.

[26]Michael I. Norton, Elizabeth W. Dunn, and Lara B. Aknin, "Spending Money on Others Promotes Happiness," *Science* 319, no. 5870 (2008): 1687-88.

[27]Kevin Yan, personal communication with Peter Greer, July 24, 2024.

[28]Crouch, "Detoxing From The Power of Money Over Our Life," 02:33-03:28.

[29]This resource is adapted from Randy Alcorn, *The Treasure Principle* (Colorado Springs, CO: Multnomah, 2001), 101, and The Finish Line Pledge Calculator, available online at www.finishlinepledge.com/calculator.

5. THE PURSUIT OF PLEASURE

[1] Unlike the other leaders profiled in this book, Tony made no professions of faith, as far as we are aware. While plenty of Christian leaders share Tony's pursuit of pleasure, we selected his story for its broad applicability and glaring similarities to Solomon's.

[2] Kai Ryssdal, "Zappos CEO Tony Hsieh: Full Interview Transcript," *Marketplace*, August 19, 2010, www.marketplace.org/2010/08/19/zappos-ceo-tony-hsieh -full-interview-transcript/.

[3] Angel Au-Yeung and David Jeans, "Tony Hsieh's American Tragedy: The Self-Destructive Last Months of the Zappos Visionary," *Forbes*, December 7, 2020, www .forbes.com/sites/angelauyeung/2020/12/04/tony-hsiehs-american-tragedy-the-self -destructive-last-months-of-the-zappos-visionary/.

[4] Sarah Todd, "The lessons of Tony Hsieh's quest for employee happiness," *Quartz*, December 1, 2020, https://qz.com/work/1940236/zappos-tony-hsieh-wanted -employees-to-be-happy-was-that-wrong.

[5] Todd, "The lessons of Tony Hsieh's quest."

[6] Au-Yeung and Jeans, "Tony Hsieh's American Tragedy."

[7] Au-Yeung and Jeans, "Tony Hsieh's American Tragedy."

[8] Kirsten Grind and Katherine Sayre, "How 'delivering happiness' failed Zappos CEO Tony Hsieh," *Marketplace*, March 15, 2022, www.marketplace.org/2022/03 /15/how-delivering-happiness-failed-zappos-ceo-tony-hsieh/.

[9] "'My Friend's Not OK,' Friends, Documents Detail Las Vegas Entrepreneur Tony Hsieh's Final Months Alive," *KLAS-TV 8NewsNow*, November 14, 2023, www.8newsnow.com/video/my-friends-not-ok-friends-documents-detail-las-vegas -entrepreneur-tony-hsiehs-final-months-alive/9173561/.

[10] Au-Yeung and Jeans, "Tony Hsieh's American Tragedy."

[11] Ryssdal, "Zappos CEO Tony Hsieh."

[12] Al Hsu, "Why We Watch Anyway," *Faith Works*, Jan-Feb 1999, 7-8.

[13] Elise Hu and Audrey Nguyen, "Too Much Pleasure Can Lead to Addiction. How to Break the Cycle and Find Balance," *NPR: Life Kit*, April 4, 2022, www.npr .org/2022/03/31/1090009509/addiction-how-to-break-the-cycle-and-find-balance.

[14] Arthur C. Brooks, "Choose Enjoyment Over Pleasure," *Atlantic*, March 24, 2022, www.theatlantic.com/family/archive/2022/03/enjoyment-not-pleasure-creates -happiness/627583/.

[15] Simon Sekles, *The Poetry of the Talmud* (New York: Published by the author, 1880), 67-68.

[16] Dan Gilbert, "The Surprising Science of Happiness," *TED*, February 2004, www .ted.com/talks/dan_gilbert_asks_why_are_we_happy/transcript#t-156000.

[17] George Müller, *The Life of Trust: Being A Narrative of the Lord's Dealings with George Müller*, ed. Herman Lincoln Wayland (Boston: Gould and Lincoln, 1868), 206.

[18]Shawn J. Wilhite, *The Didache: A Commentary* (Eugene, OR: Cascade Books, 2019), xxxvii.

[19]Father Mario Attard, "Lent with the Fathers of the Church and Some Spiritual Writers," *Catholic Insight*, March 9, 2022, https://catholicinsight.com/lent-with-the-fathers-of-the-church-and-some-spiritual-writers/.

[20]Dan Williams, interview with Jill Heisey, August 27, 2024.

[21]Douglas McKelvey, "Feasting with Friends" in *Every Moment Holy: Volume 1*, pocket ed. (Nashville, TN: Rabbit Room Press, 2019), 120.

6. THE PROBLEM WITH POWER

[1]Britannica online, "John Emerich Edward Dalberg Acton, 1st Baron," accessed December 6, 2024, www.britannica.com/biography/John-Emerich-Edward-Dalberg-Acton-1st-Baron-Acton.

[2]Daniel Silliman, "Died: Gospel for Asia Founder Athanasius Yohannan," *Christianity Today*, May 9, 2024, www.christianitytoday.com/news/2024/may/kp-athanasius-yohannan-gospel-asia-founder-died.html.

[3]"Testimony of Joe and Cari P.," GFA Diaspora, www.gfadiaspora.com/testimony-of-jp-cp—1999-01-16.

[4]"Our Concerns," GFA Diaspora, www.gfadiaspora.com/our-concerns.

[5]"Testimony of Troy and Pam," GFA Diaspora, www.gfadiaspora.com/wp-content/uploads/2015/04/TroyPam-Testimony-with-no-last-names.pdf.

[6]"Testimony of Cassie," GFA Diaspora, www.gfadiaspora.com/testimonies-2.

[7]"Evidence Supporting False Teaching on Authority," GFA Diaspora, www.gfadiaspora.com/wp-content/uploads/2015/04/Pats-ordination-with-no-last-names.pdf.

[8]"Receiving Honor from Men," GFA Diaspora, www.gfadiaspora.com/receiving-honor-from-men.

[9]"Testimony of Eric and Natalie," GFA Diaspora, www.gfadiaspora.com/testimony-of-eric-and-natalie—1999-01-19.

[10]"Our Concerns: GFA Leadership Practices and Teaches a False View of Spiritual Authority," GFA Diaspora, www.gfadiaspora.com/our-concerns.

[11]Warren Throckmorton, "The Other Gospel for Asia Report K. P. Yohannan Did Not Want Anyone to Read," December 11, 2015, https://wthrockmorton.com/2015/12/11/the-other-gospel-for-asia-report-you-should-read.

[12]"Books of 1–2 Kings Summary," *The Bible Project*, accessed December 7, 2024, https://bibleproject.com/explore/video/kings/.

[13]Andy Crouch, "It's Time to Talk about Power," *Christianity Today*, October, 2013, www.christianitytoday.com/ct/2013/october/andy-crouch-its-time-to-talk-about-power.html.

[14]"Recognitions," Marshalling Resources, accessed December 7, 2024, https://www.marshallingresources.com/cyntmarshall.

[15]Cynt Marshall, *You've Been Chosen* (New York: Ballantine Books, 2022), 83.

[16]Jenny Luna, "Cynt Marshall: Workplace Culture as a Measure of Success," Stanford Graduate School of Business, February 23, 2023, www.gsb.stanford.edu/insights /cynt-marshall-workplace-culture-measure-success.

[17]Carl Combs, "Reflections," *A Life Well Lived: A Farewell Tribute*, accessed December 7, 2024, www.cru.org/content/dam/cru/about/bill-bright-memorial/life_lived_well.pdf.

[18]"Manual Labor," *Subiaco Abbey*, accessed December 7, 2024, https://countrymonks .org/labora.

[19]Andrew Murray, *Humility: The Beauty of Holiness*, second ed. (London: James Nisbet & Co., 1896), 35.

7. THE QUEST FOR CONTROL

[1]Carey Nieuwhof, "Trusting in God: Are You Trusting in God or Being Foolish?," Carey Nieuwhof (blog), October 29, 2024, https://careynieuwhof.com/can-tell -whether-risk-means-youre-trusting-god-being-stupid/.

[2]Joni Eareckson Tada, interview by Peter Greer and Jill Heisey, February 2, 2023.

[3]Joni Eareckson Tada, *Seeking God: My Journey of Prayer and Praise* (Brentwood, TN: Wolgemuth & Hyatt, 1991), 3.

[4]Joni Eareckson Tada, "January 2" in *Diamonds in the Dust* (Grand Rapids, MI: Zondervan, 1993).

[5]"Joni and Friends President Laura Gardner Announces Her Role Change," Joni and Friends, October 8, 2024, https://joniandfriends.org/press-releases/joni-and-friends -president-laura-gardner-announces-her-role-change/.

[6]Tada, interview by Greer and Heisey, February 2, 2023.

[7]Tada, interview by Greer and Heisey, February 2, 2023.

[8]Tada, interview by Greer and Heisey, February 2, 2023.

[9]Dave Blanchard, "2023 Praxis Community Letter," *Praxis Journal*, May 23, 2023, https://journal.praxis.co/2023-praxis-community-letter-808853307dc.

[10]Sharon Hodde Miller, *The Cost of Control: Why We Crave It, the Anxiety It Gives Us, and the Real Power God Promises* (Minneapolis, MN: Baker Publishing Group, 2022), 130.

[11]Louie Giglio, Facebook, December 14, 2020, www.facebook.com/officialLouie Giglio/posts/worship-and-worry-cannot-occupy-the-same-space-they-cant-both-fill -our-mouths-at/1728041937371842/.

[12]Leif Hass, "How Awe Can Help Us Through Tough Times," *Greater Good Magazine*, July 24, 2023, https://greatergood.berkeley.edu/article/item/how_awe_can_help_us _through_tough_times.

[13]Hass, "How Awe Can Help Us Through Tough Times."

[14]Elizabeth Bernstein, "The Science of Prayer," *Wall Street Journal*, May 17, 2020, www .wsj.com/articles/the-science-of-prayer-11589720400.

[15]Bernstein, "The Science of Prayer."

8. THE NEED FOR SPEED

[1] Jason Russell, "Kony 2012," *Invisible Children*, accessed September 12, 2024, https://youtu.be/Y4MnpzG5Sqc?si=jgyVenF4D9sESKvg.

[2] "Jason Russell on Kony 2012 Going Viral," *Oprah's Next Chapter*, October 4, 2012, www.youtube.com/watch?v=sYbnQlltJ2w.

[3] "Jason Russell Explains the Pressure He Felt," *Oprah's Next Chapter*, October 8, 2012, https://youtu.be/dADUMe_3h3g?si=rFjMTcEvZjlTdMVu.

[4] "What Jason Russell Remembers About His Breakdown," *Oprah's Next Chapter*, October 8, 2012, www.youtube.com/watch?v=Q7MCh19igW4.

[5] "How Have Things Changed Since Kony 2012?," *Invisible Children*, March 16, 2017, https://invisiblechildren.com/blog/2017/03/16/five-years-kony-2012.

[6] Carl Jung, as quoted in John Ortberg, "Ruthlessly Eliminate Hurry," *Christianity Today*, July 4, 2002, www.christianitytoday.com/2002/07/cln20704/.

[7] John Ortberg, "Ruthlessly Eliminate Hurry," *Leadership Journal*, July 4, 2002, www.christianitytoday.com/2002/07/cln20704/.

[8] Alan Fadling, personal correspondence with the authors, December 9, 2024.

[9] Henry M. Morris, "Sweet Naamah," *Days of Praise,* Institute for Creation Research, February 14, 2024, www.icr.org/article/sweet-naamah.

[10] Philip D. Stern, "Solomon's Egyptian Bride: Artful Alliance or Biblical Boast?," *Biblical Archaeology Review,* Spring 2024, https://library.biblicalarchaeology.org/department/solomons-egyptian-bride-artful-alliance-or-biblical-boast/.

[11] *EA 4 in The Amarna Letters*, trans. William L. Moran (Baltimore: Johns Hopkins University Press, 1992), 8-9.

[12] Blaise Pascal, *Pensées*, trans. A. J. Krailsheimer (London: Penguin Classics, 1995), 37-38.

[13] Douglas Rushkoff, *Present Shock* (New York: Current, 2013), 2.

[14] Doublas Rushkoff, personal correspondence with the authors, November 1, 2024.

[15] Anonymous advance reader, personal correspondence with the authors, November 15, 2024.

[16] A. J. Swoboda, *Subversive Sabbath* (Grand Rapids, MI: Brazos, 2018), 5.

[17] John Mark Comer, "John Mark Comer Teachings Podcast: Rest for Your Soul podcast, Sabbath Episode 1," August 12, 2022, https://podcasts.apple.com/us/podcast/rest-for-your-soul-sabbath-e1/id1592847144?i=1000575858186.

[18] Adele Ahlberg Calhoun, *Spiritual Disciplines Handbook*, rev. ed. (Downers Grove, IL: InterVarsity Press, 2015), 44.

[19] Wayne Muller, *Sabbath* (New York: Bantam, 2000), 1.

[20] Paul B. Brown, "Are You Focused Enough? (A Surprising Case Study)," *Forbes*, May 10, 2012, www.forbes.com/sites/actiontrumpseverything/2012/05/10/are-you-focused-enough-a-surprising-case-study.

9. THE ISLAND EFFECT

[1] Kate Shellnutt and Sarah Eekhoff Zylstra, "Ravi Zacharias Responds to Sexting Allegations, Credentials Critique," *Christianity Today*, December 3, 2017, www .christianitytoday.com/2017/12/ravi-zacharias-sexting-extortion-lawsuit-doctorate -bio-rzim/.

[2] Daniel Silliman and Kate Shellnutt, "Ravi Zacharias Hid Hundreds of Pictures of Women, Abuse During Massages, and a Rape Allegation," *Christianity Today*, February 11, 2021, www.christianitytoday.com/2021/02/ravi-zacharias-rzim-investigation -sexual-abuse-sexting-rape/.

[3] Edmund Chan, "'See You Later, Ravi Zacharias!': A Tribute from a Friend of the Famed Christian Apologist," *Salt&Light*, May 22, 2020, https://saltandlight.sg/news /see-you-later-ravi-zacharias-a-tribute-from-a-friend-of-the-famed-christian-apologist.

[4] This article has been removed from *Salt&Light*'s website but remains accessible through online archives. Edmund Chan, "Ravi Zacharias: How Does a Shocked and Grieving World Respond?," *Salt&Light*, February 14, 2021, https://web.archive .org/web/20210214130221/https://saltandlight.sg/news/ravi-zacharias-how-does-a -shocked-and-grieving-world-respond/.

[5] Lynsey M. Barron and William P. Eiselstein, "Report of Independent Investigation into Sexual Misconduct of Ravi Zacharias," Miller & Martin PPLC, February 9, 2021, www.courthousenews.com/wp-content/uploads/2021/02/zacharias-report.pdf.

[6] Carey Nieuwhof, "6 Reasons You Feel Lonely In Leadership," accessed December 7, 2024, https://careynieuwhof.com/6-reasons-you-feel-lonely-in-leadership/.

[7] This letter has been removed from RZIM's website but remains accessible through online archives. "Open Letter from the International Board of Directors of RZIM on the Investigation of Ravi Zacharias," RZIM, February 11, 2021, https://web.archive .org/web/20210211224520/www.rzim.org/read/rzim-updates/board-statement.

[8] Mark DeMoss, "Lessons from Evangelicalism's PR Guru," *Christianity Today*, April 2019, www.christianitytoday.com/2019/03/mark-demoss-evangelical-public -relations-firm-closing-lesso/.

[9] "Leadership Standard Insights Report," ECFA, accessed December 7, 2024, www. ecfa.org/LeadershipStandard.aspx.

[10] Priscilla Shirer, "Priscilla Shirer: How Church Leaders Can Seek Mentorship and Accountability," interview by Ed Stetzer and Daniel Yang on *The Stetzer ChurchLeaders Podcast*, August 7, 2024, https://churchleaders.com/podcast/491149-priscilla-shirer -church-leaders-mentorship-accountability.html.

[11] Richard J. Foster, *Celebration of Discipline* (New York: HarperSanFrancisco, 1998), 146.

[12] Dietrich Bonhoeffer, *Life Together*, trans. John W. Doberstein (New York: Harper & Row, 1954), 112.

[13] Bonhoeffer, *Life Together*, 116.

[14] Andy Crouch, as quoted in Katelyn Beaty, *Celebrities for Jesus* (Grand Rapids, MI: Brazos, 2022), 172.

[15] The idea of Constellation Mentoring was originally introduced to me through the book *Connecting* by Paul D. Stanley and J. Robert Clinton (Colorado Springs, CO: NavPress, 1992).

10. SELF AT THE CENTER

[1] For a detailed examination, we recommend the Christianity Today podcast *The Rise and Fall of Mars Hill*, https://www.christianitytoday.com/podcasts /the-rise-and-fall-of-mars-hill/.

[2] Sarah Eekhoff Zylstra, "Seattle Reboot: Life After Mars Hill," *The Gospel Coalition*, May 30, 2017, www.thegospelcoalition.org/article/seattle-reboot-life-after -mars-hill/.

[3] Zylstra, "Seattle Reboot."

[4] Timothy Keller, *The Freedom of Self-Forgetfulness: The Path to True Christian Joy* (LaGrange, KY: 10Publishing, 2012), 32.

[5] Julie Roys, "Tim Keller: Megachurches Are 'Poor Places for Formation' & Have 'Addictive Dependence' on Founders," *The Roys Report*, April 7, 2022, https://julieroys .com/tim-keller-megachurches-poor-places-formation/.

[6] "Succession Planning for Nonprofits/Managing Leadership Transitions," National Council of Nonprofits, accessed December 7, 2024, www.councilofnon profits.org/running-nonprofit/governance-leadership/succession-planning-non profits-managing-leadership.

[7] Roys, "Tim Keller: Megachurches Are 'Poor Places for Formation.'"

[8] Libbie Landles-Cobb, Kirk Kramer, and Katie Smith Milway, "The Nonprofit Leadership Development Deficit," *Stanford Social Innovation Review*, October 22, 2015, https://ssir.org/articles/entry/the_nonprofit_leadership_development_deficit.

[9] Susan Brown, personal conversation with Peter Greer, September 6, 2024.

CONCLUSION: FEW FINISH WELL

[1] Henri J. M. Nouwen, *In the Name of Jesus: Reflections on Christian Leadership* (London: Darton, Longman and Todd, 1989).

[2] Gerald Griffin, "Into the Wilderness," Bridgetown Church, February 26, 2017, accessed September 13, 2024, https://bridgetown.church/teachings/gospel-of-matthew /into-the-wilderness.

[3] Mark DeMoss, *The Little Red Book of Wisdom*, updated and expanded ed. (Nashville, TN: Nelson, 2023), 191.

ABOUT THE AUTHORS

PETER GREER

Peter is the president and CEO of HOPE International, a global Christ-centered economic development organization serving throughout Africa, Asia, Latin America, and Eastern Europe. Prior to joining HOPE, Peter worked internationally as a microfinance adviser in Cambodia and Zimbabwe and as managing director for Urwego Bank in Rwanda. He received a BS in international business from Messiah University and an MPP in political and economic development from Harvard's Kennedy School. Peter's favorite part of his job is spending time with the entrepreneurs HOPE serves—whether harvesting coffee with farmers in Rwanda, dancing alongside savings groups in Haiti, or visiting the greenhouses of entrepreneurs in Ukraine. As an advocate for the church's role in missions and alleviating extreme poverty, Peter has coauthored over fifteen books, including *Lead with Prayer* (ECPA bestseller), *Mission Drift* (selected as a Book Award Winner from Christianity Today), *Rooting for Rivals* (selected as a Leadership Resource of the Year in *Outreach* magazine), *The Spiritual Danger of Doing Good* (selected as one of the top forty books on poverty by *WORLD* magazine), and *Created to Flourish* (which his mom reviewed with five stars and a smiley face emoji). More important than his role at HOPE is his role as husband to Laurel and dad to their four children. While his sports loyalties remain in New England, Peter and his family live in Lancaster, Pennsylvania.

JILL HEISEY

Jill Heisey is a writer who is passionate about helping leaders and nonprofits share their stories. She's collaborated on the books *Lead with Prayer*, *Rooting for Rivals*, and *The Gift of Disillusionment* as well as the children's book *Keza Paints a Bright Future* and has written for Christianity Today's Better Samaritan blog. Jill graduated from Messiah University with degrees in politics and Spanish and resides outside Washington, DC, with her husband, Bryan, and their two daughters.

"Peter Greer and Jill Heisey have written a timely and highly relevant book that is a must-read for Christian leaders. In *How Leaders Lose Their Way*, they illuminate the motivations and intentions of the heart and the never-ending pull on them. This book is a clarion call to wake up, search your heart, repent, and return to the center of God's will for kingdom calling and service. The ongoing challenges remain to start, sustain, scale, and grow the impact of Christ-centered nonprofits. But it is only possible if we faithfully follow God's way to accomplish the task. This book will guide you!"

Tami Heim, president and CEO of Christian Leadership Alliance

"Too many leaders drive by feel through life, mistaking inertia and intention for direction and destination. Legacies are lost when not lived. *How Leaders Lose Their Way* is a lighthouse in the night, shining needed lights to prevent unforced errors and disasters on the predictable hazards. It's not if we will struggle with drift but how we will respond. The insights, resources, wisdom, and case studies of this book can change the win rate of leaders. May it be so!"

Mike Sharrow, CEO of C12 Business Forums

"We're all devastated when leaders don't finish well. But how often do we hold up the mirror to see that we're all at risk of drifting and do something about it? Thank you, Peter Greer and Jill Heisey, for revealing the common warning signs of leadership drift and for challenging us with wise strategies rooted in humility to help us finish well."

Michael Martin, president and CEO of the Evangelical Council for Financial Accountability

"This book offers a perfect pairing of timeless wisdom and timely truth, all wonderfully told. It reminds that leadership is not only a matter of strategy and skill but foremost about our longings and loves. Though often unnamed, these deeper currents set our trajectory far more than our claimed values and mission statements. They inevitably shape the organizations we lead and the people we become. So we do well to search out these matters of the heart, as this volume helps us do, asking God for the unmatched gladness that comes only as double-mindedness is turned to purity of heart."

Jedd Medefind, president of the Christian Alliance for Orphans

"When leaders drift, mission drifts. Grounded in Scripture and case studies of biblical and contemporary leaders, *How Leaders Lose Their Way* equips leaders to recognize potential areas of drift, while providing practical tools and practices to stay focused on priorities and purpose. This book is a must-read for ministry leaders and organizational leaders who are committed to finishing well!"

Tom Lin, president and CEO of InterVarsity Christian Fellowship/USA

"I *devoured* this book. *How Leaders Lose Their Way* is both a sobering warning and a hopeful guide—an invitation to finish the race of leadership with integrity and joy. Peter Greer and Jill Heisey have given us a masterpiece of clarity, conviction, and grace, showing that drift is subtle but faithfulness is possible. Page after page left me convicted, encouraged, and—most importantly—anchored to the One who keeps us mission true."

Jordan Raynor, author of *The Sacredness of Secular Work* and *Redeeming Your Time*

"No author outside Scripture has contributed to the culture of our ministry more than Peter Greer. The lessons in *How Leaders Lose Their Way* are critical for all Christian leaders who are seeking to create lasting impact for the kingdom. What a wonderful gift to the church!"
Joel Penton, founder and CEO of LifeWise Academy

"Organizational leadership is a distinct privilege, but it also sets traps for the human heart. In their book *How Leaders Lose Their Way*, Peter Greer and Jill Heisey do a wonderful job of illuminating these traps and pointing the way toward dealing with them. Their approach invites leaders to reflect on how they are drifting and sets out practical steps forward. It's a refreshing and much-needed reminder that leadership isn't just about what we accomplish but who we become in the process."
Mike Bontrager, founder and CEO of Square Roots Collective

"Cogent, clear, and convicting! *How Leaders Lose Their Way* is a must-read for leaders in churches and Christian organizations. This is a vital sequel to *Mission Drift* (by Peter Greer and others), as it probes the personal drift that so easily occurs in positions of power. And significantly, it points not just to the problems but provides spiritual resources for amending our ways."
Dennis Hollinger, president emeritus and senior distinguished professor of Christian ethics at Gordon-Conwell Theological Seminary

"Long-term faithfulness in leadership often seems to be the exception rather than the norm. The pressures, temptations, and challenges leaders face can slowly erode our integrity and purpose, often without our realizing it—until it's too late. Personally, *How Leaders Lose Their Way* proved to be challenging and at times convicting. Ultimately it caused me to pause and evaluate my life and my decisions, all the while asking God to guide and help me realign my path where I have strayed. If you want to finish well, this book is a must-read!"
David Ashcraft, president and CEO of Global Leadership Network and author of *What Was I Thinking?*

"A compelling, profound, and powerful word for these days, boldly naming the temptations and courageously giving examples both current and biblical . . . and at the same time, giving examples of hope to avoid the pitfalls. The exercises at the end of each chapter give opportunity for self-reflection and work through Scripture and prayer. This is also *How NOT to Lose Your Way*. Absolutely a necessary read for all current leaders and aspiring leaders. A seminal book that is timeless."
Jo Anne Lyon, general superintendent emerita of The Wesleyan Church

"Mission-driven leaders often manage their organizations and teams with more attention and diligence than their own lives. Peter Greer and Jill Heisey remind us with urgency and clarity that a failure to do so can end in the ultimate tragedy of both, and that as builders and leaders, we must mind our own practices and hearts from which we work and serve the world. We cannot be reminded of this too often, and this book is a key resource for us in that lifelong journey."
Dave Blanchard, cofounder and CEO of Praxis

Like this book?

Scan the code to discover more content like this!

Get on IVP's email list to receive special offers, exclusive book news, and thoughtful content from your favorite authors on topics you care about.

ivp | InterVarsity Press